D1649549

Hidden
TENERIFE

CONNY MELKEBEEK

withdrawn from stock

INTRODUCTION

HIDDEN TENERIFE isn't an ordinary guide to Tenerife: the aim of this book is to help you discover wonderful places on the island outside of the mainstream tourist circuit. Some inevitable popular must-see locations are included as well, but in that case you'll get to know these places from an insider's perspective, so your visit can become a more memorable one.

The island's most popular resorts may offer many pleasant surprises, however, getting to know the 'real' Tenerife requires some exploring outside of these tourist zones. This guide will lead you to inspiring areas where one is able to experience the local life and enjoy the island's breathtaking nature, the stunning ravines, the many volcanoes and the distant beaches. At the same time it will also tell you where to eat the tastiest food and savour the best of wines while helping you locate original bars, shops, galleries, museums, squares, parks and lots of other unique places. Holidays are all about undertaking exciting and fun activities, so we have also included many unusual experiences such as kayaking in transparent boats, exploring a volcanic tube, bathing in lava pools, sliding down forest ziplines, diving to the bottom of the ocean or gliding above the mountains on a kite.

Finally it's good to know that this book doesn't try to provide a complete overview on what to see or do in Tenerife. We recommend treating this guide as a good friend who knows the island well and wants to give you a fabulous time on the little piece of paradise you have chosen to visit.

HOW TO USE THIS BOOK

The idea behind this book is to list the places the author would recommend to a friend who wants to get to know Tenerife intimately. It encourages you to explore more remote locations on the island and to go on unexpected adventures in the wild natural surroundings. It also helps you find the most authentic restaurants and places to shop – places where you will meet the warm-hearted locals.

The guide is divided in different chapters that correspond with different regions on the island, except for the first one, which serves as a general introduction and is interesting to read wherever you plan to spend time in Tenerife. Every chapter includes a map to help you get oriented. The maps that cover a larger region – in chapters 3 (the North), 4 (Mount Teide) and 5 (the South) – have a large scale and aren't detailed enough to determine exact locations. They do give you a sense of direction and distance and are handy in combination with your GPS or road map. The map of Santa Cruz has a smaller scale, but you will also need a smartphone to locate a specific address, or a detailed city map (which you can obtain from any tourist office or in most hotels).

In the following chapters you will find things to experience and locations to visit, as well as the addresses of a number of shops, bars, hotels and restaurants. Please bear in mind that businesses change all the time, so the chef who hits a high note one day might be uninspiring the night you visit, or the bar considered the place to be to meet locals, may be calm on the night you're there. This is obviously a highly personal selection. You might not always agree with it. If you want to leave a comment, recommend a restaurant or reveal your favourite place on the island, please get in touch: visit *www.lusterweb.com* or e-mail *info@lusterweb.com*.

ABOUT THE AUTHOR

Belgian-Scottish C O N N Y M E L K E B E E K studied at the university of Ghent but later moved to Tenerife; she has been living and working there for more than 25 years now. What started out as a seasonal assignment while working for a tour operator, later became her life. Conny is now self-employed as an official tourist guide; her job brings her to every corner of the island and leads to new discoveries every day. After all these years, Conny is still endlessly fascinated by the natural beauty of the surroundings, and she very much enjoys hiking along the countless paths and exploring new secret places. In her free time she practises yoga and studies Mandarin – a challenging hobby she loves. With her partner Jaak she shares the desire to see the world and experience other cultures.

The author wishes to thank the many people who helped her create this guide. Special thanks goes out to Lourdes and Justy for sharing their extensive knowledge on good places to eat, to Isabel Mora for her valuable advice about the art scene, to Isabel Herteleer and Matias who helped researching the parts on Santa Cruz, to Claudia for her encouragement, to Helena and Laura who shared a lot about La Laguna and to the supportive Dettie at Luster. More people who contributed with their tips and advice are Rolf Fuchs, Tomás Salazar, Mariano Vercesi, Ellen Baert, the girls at the Tui office, Mandy, Belky, Olga, Paulette, Tere and Eloy. And last but not least Conny's thanks goes out to her daughter Ornella and to Ornella's grandmother Ignacia Candelaria Torres de Vera, who represent the Canarian side of the family.

CONTENT

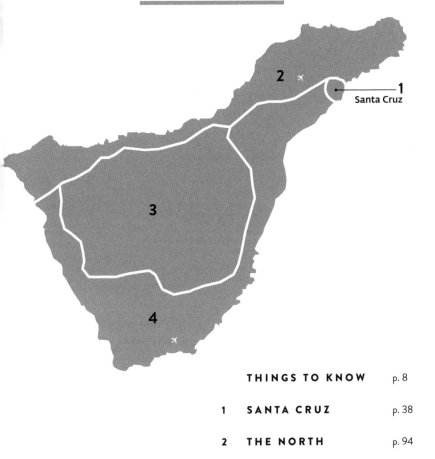

Santa Cruz

1

2

3

4

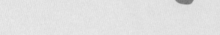

A El Hierro
B La Palma
C La Gomera
D **Tenerife**
E Gran Canaria
F Fuerteventura
G Lanzarote

Canary Islands

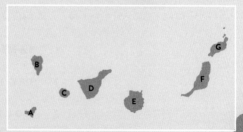

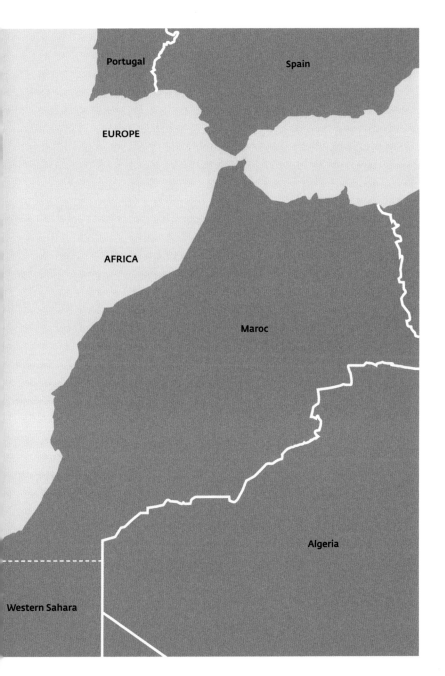

THINGS TO KNOW

With its 2034 square kilometres, Tenerife is the largest of the seven Canary Islands. Although its population is below the one million mark, in recent years the island annually receives around 5,7 million visitors. Many of these guests want to jump into their beachwear as quickly as possible and bask in the sun for the remainder of their stay. Luckily for them the island offers a wide array of beaches, coves, resort pools and natural pools to fully savour the all-year-round warm and sunny days.

On the other hand, those willing to explore the territory will be astounded by the marvels of this beautiful subtropical island. Not only will you encounter the most dramatic volcanic landscapes, but also the most exclusive and remarkable fauna and flora, traditional little mountain villages where time hasn't moved on, breathtaking mountain views, singular starry skies, colourful colonial towns exposing centuries of history, world-class museums and bustling markets inviting you to cheerfully linger.

Best of all though are the authentic, warm-hearted, joyful and easy-going Canarian people you will meet. Their acclaimed love for good food and fine wine is considerable and you are in for some extraordinary culinary adventures. On a daily basis Canarios are happy to share their island and their culture, their fiestas, their gastronomy and their general joie-de-vivre. And although you may not speak the lingo, if you offer any *Tinerfeño* a genuine smile, you are most likely to receive an even bigger one in return.

HIGOS PICOS OR PRICKLY PEARS

EAT

DRINK

DISCOVER

CULTURE

RANDOM

Local **SOUL FOOD**

1 **COSTILLAS CON PAPAS Y PIÑA**

Three main ingredients turn this traditional dish into one of the islanders' favourites: corn on the cob, potatoes and pork ribs. The secret lies in the slow cooking of the previously desalted ribs, making the meat as tender as lard. Always accompanied by a tasty *mojo cilantro* (Canarian coriander sauce).

2 **POTAJE CANARIO**

The southern diet, adapted to hot weather, often differs from the menu in the North where temperatures are lower. But no matter where you are, a hearty plate of *potaje Canario* always works wonders at feeding the soul. *Potaje de berros* (thick watercress soup) or *potaje de lentejas* (thick lentil soup) are both excellent choices.

3 **ESCALDÓN DE GOFIO**

Gofio is flour made from toasted cereals and prepared sweet as well as savoury. It is eaten on a daily basis in many Canarian households. To make an *escaldón,* mix the *gofio* with a rich meat broth and add bits of meat and vegetables to taste. The final touch is a drizzle of green or spicy red *mojo* sauce on the surface.

4 PAPAS ARRUGADAS CON MOJO

The Canary Islands are the only place in Europe where you'll find a variety of the original 'Andean potatoes'. Called *papas negras* or *papas bonitas*, they're considered a gastronomical treasure. Cooked in the skin with lots of sea salt makes them *arrugadas* or wrinkled. Combined with the typical *mojo* sauces, they are very addictive.

4 PAPAS ARRUGADAS

Interesting **TYPES OF FRUIT**

---

5 **HIGO PICO OR PRICKLY PEAR**

This is the spiky fruit from the Mexican *opuntia spp cactus*. The cactus itself is host to the cochineal, an insect from which the red dye E-120 is extracted. At its peak of exploitation in 1870, thousands of kilos of cochineal were exported, before entering in crisis with the arrival of artificial colorants. Nowadays no one bothers about the beasties, but enjoys the lovely refreshing cactus fruit, ready in summer and rich in vitamin C.

6 PLÁTANO CANARIO

6 **PLÁTANO CANARIO** The banana is the most important crop of the archipelago. The Canarian bananas are the only ones in the world to carry the PGI (Protected Geographical Indication) quality seal. Sweeter and more moist than other varieties, they are left longer on the plant to mature. Don't be fooled by their brown spots: this is their typical hallmark. Full of goodness, make sure to give them a try.

7 **PAPAYAS, MANGOS AND AVOCADOS** Nicknamed 'the fortunate islands', the Canary Islands have an all-year-round average temperature of roughly 21,5 degrees Celsius with very little rainfall. Tropical fruit like papayas, mangos and avocados love it here as much as we do. Most local bars will serve *zumos* or *batidos*: divine juices, smoothies or milkshakes holding all this sunny sweetness.

The sweetest of **S W E E T S**

8 **BIENMESABE**

In the past one of the islands' crops was sugar cane, which reflects in the local gastronomy. When it comes to desserts, *Tinerfeños* love to stick to all things sweet 'made in Canarias'. Bienmesabe, originally from neighbouring island La Palma, is a rich and caloric delight made with almonds, eggs, sugar and lemon.

9 **FRANGOLLO**

An old and tasty Canarian dessert, but not readily found on menus as it is quite elaborate. Milk, maize flour, lemon, eggs, sugar, butter, raisins, almonds and cinnamon are the main ingredients. You might have to get yourself invited to a true native's home though, to enjoy a taste of it.

10 **QUESILLO CANARIO**

Quesillo Canario or Canarian style flan is one of the most delicious, incredibly rich and creamy traditional desserts. It is made with condensed milk and eggs, which ensures its firm texture and its sweet-eggy taste. Relatively simple to make at home, this is definitely a must-try that you will easily find at most typical Canarian restaurants.

C O F F E E *all kinds*

---

11 HOW TO ORDER A COFFEE

Here are some useful guidelines:
– *un café solo*: a small strong espresso coffee;
– *un cortado natural*: a small strong espresso coffee with milk;
– *un cortado leche y leche*: a small strong espresso; coffee with milk and sweet condensed milk;
– *un café con leche*: a large coffee with milk;
– *un café americano*: a large black coffee.
Good luck!

12 BARRAQUITO

Who wants Starbucks if you can have a *barraquito* instead. A mixture of sweet and robust with an irresistible flavour. A small coffee par excellence with its added condensed and natural milk, its splash of 43 liquor, some cinnamon on top and a little piece of lemon zest to give the final touch. Heavenly.

12 **BARRAQUITO**

13 **CARAJILLO**

You might call this the male version of the *barraquito*. A traditional Spanish drink, combining coffee with brandy and no milk. Whereas *barraquitos* can be enjoyed at any moment of the day, *carajillo* is rather an after-dinner digestive, and more so if you wish to go dancing afterwards.

BEER, WINE and RUM

---

14 **DORADA PILSEN**

Brewed in Santa Cruz de Tenerife, this is the most popular island beer. A 100% clear-golden malt which has been awarded internationally. Their motto is: "¡*Qué suerte vivir aquí*!" (How fortunate to live here!), which has become a humorous daily expression among residents. Check out their vibrant publicity spots on YouTube.

15 **CANARY WINES AND CHEESES**

Canary wines, among the world's best according to prominent wine guides, have been around for many centuries. William Shakespeare was a great lover of the brew and mentioned it several times in his writings. Many hours of sun, a rich volcanic soil and a great diversity of grapes have assured their international prestige. Tenerife has five designations of origin, all of excellent quality. Canary cheeses, also world-prized, make the ideal accompaniment.

16 **CANARY RUM**

The history of rum is undoubtedly related to the archipelago. Sugar cane, the raw material of rum, was taken by Columbus from the Canary Islands to the New World and later to Cuba. Rum is therefore firmly fused with Canarian culture, producing popular brands such as Arehucas, Guajiro, Cocal, etc. Also very beloved is the famous Canarian *Ron Miel* (honey rum) enjoying the protected designation of origin status.

The most **SACRED**

17 **LA VIRGEN DE LA CANDELARIA**
Plaza de la
Candelaria
Candelaria

La Virgen de la Candelaria, a delicate black Madonna with child on her arm, is the patron saint of the seven Canary Islands. Housed in the Basilica of Candelaria, she is the most beloved statue of Tenerife. Cloaked in fabulous gowns, she first appeared on the island in the 15th century. On August 15th, pilgrims from every corner of the island walk to Candelaria to pay tribute.

18 **EL SANTÍSIMO CRISTO DE LA LAGUNA**
Plaza San Francisco
La Laguna
cristodelalaguna.org

A fine Flemish, late-Gothic statue of Christ, brought to La Laguna in 1520 by the conqueror Alonso Fernández de Lugo. The centuries-old deep devotion for this Christ is quite impressive. Every year on September 14th and in his honour, huge crowds gather at the Plaza del Cristo to attend the biggest, deafening fireworks display on the island.

19 **SANTO HERMANO PEDRO**
TF-643
El Médano

Canonised in 2002 by Pope John Paul II, Brother Pedro was born in Vilaflor in 1626. He herded goats and lived in a cave near El Médano. After deciding to move to Guatemala, he dedicated his life to the needy and established a new order, the Bethlehemites. The Saint, who is said to have worked many miracles, is venerated at his cave sanctuary, full of gifts and candles.

17 **LA VIRGEN DE LA CANDELARIA**

Have fun while you **LEARN**

20 FINCA LAS MARGARITAS, BANANA EXPERIENCE

Av. La Calma, Ctra
Guaza TF-66
Las Galletas
+34 617 696 045
*fincalasmargaritas
lasgalletas.blogspot.
com.es*

Here you will have a unique opportunity to find out what really happens behind the block walls and the netting near the coasts. The tour on this active banana plantation is mainly self-guided, with a short talk and some product sampling at the end of it. Try to go on a Tuesday, as this is their harvest day.

21 SAN BLAS ENVIRONMENTAL RESERVE

Av. de Greñamora
1, Urb. San Blas
Los Abrigos
+34 922 749 010
*sandos.com/
sandos-san-blas/
environmental-
reserve*

The eco-friendly San Blas Hotel offers a two-hour entertaining and well-researched tour through the San Blas Environmental Reserve. Featuring enactments of real life characters, the island's history, geology and nature are explained. Nice pools and a mini spa are also available. End your day with a tasty fresh fish lunch in nearby Los Abrigos.

20 FINCA LAS MARGARITAS

22 SPOTTING WHALES AND DOLPHINS

Puerto Colón dock 5
Costa Adeje
+34 626 002 205
oceanbluetenerife.
com

Besides the resident colony of pilot whales and dolphins, migrating whales annually swim past Tenerife. Catamarans, glass-bottom boats and traditional wooden vessels run various whale and dolphin-watching trips. Opt for smaller boats as you'll get better close-up views. Although slightly pricier, they're less crowded and offer more personalised attention.

23 VOLCANIC TUBE: CUEVA DEL VIENTO

C/ Los Piquetes 51
Icod de los Vinos
+34 922 815 339
cuevadelviento.net

Explore the entrails of the earth and learn all about volcanism on Tenerife. See how lava tubes are formed and the ecosystems that exist inside of them. The cave tour takes around 60 minutes and sturdy shoes are a must. Not for children under 5, but older children will love it. Groups are kept small, so pre-book and buy your tickets online.

22 SPOTTING WHALES AND DOLPHINS

Exceptional **TRADITIONS**

24 **SEMANA SANTA PROCESSIONS**
40 days after
Ash Wednesday
La Laguna

During Easter at La Laguna, religious fervour takes over the entire city. Processions, among the most celebrated in Spain, reunite fraternities and brotherhoods, who carry holy images through the streets. The evening silent parade is rather awe-inspiring, even for non-believers.

25 **DAY OF THE CROSS**
May 3rd
Santa Cruz

A great day for Santa Cruz, following a tradition that is rooted in the founding of the city 500 years ago. The capital dawns with a display of crosses, strikingly adorned with flowers in thousands of shades. Many neighbourhoods compete for the title of the most imposing cross.

26 **SAND AND FLOWER CARPETS**
coincides with
Corpus Christi
La Orotava

In La Orotava, an 900-square-metre sand carpet, strewn with more or less 1300 kg sand from the National Park, covers the Town Hall square entirely. This beautiful piece of art is extremely impressive. The surrounding streets are equally adorned with petals, leaves and pine needles. All is kept in place until the Corpus Christi procession is allowed to pass.

27 BATHING OF THE GOATS

June 24th
Puerto de la Cruz

One by one, around one thousand goats and twenty horses, take a dip in the sea at the port of Puerto de la Cruz. This is an ancestral practice related to fertility and inherited from the original inhabitants called Guanches. Get there early in the morning to fully enjoy this very exceptional tradition.

28 WOODEN BOARDS OF SAN ANDRÉS

November 29th
Icod de los Vinos

This is the night when wineries are opened and the new wine, accompanied with roasted chestnuts and salted fish, is tasted. Under the watchful eye of onlookers, the daring young of Icod de los Vinos slide down the steepest cobbled streets, seated on greased wooden boards gathering maximum speed. A fun night out.

G O L F *under the sun*

29 9 GOLF COURSES
+34 922 237 521
*webtenerife.com/
tenerifegolf*

Even the most particular golfer will be satisfied with a choice of nine spectacular golf courses, scattered over the island and designed by people such as Severiano Ballesteros, Donald Steel or John Jacobs. Course number 10 is situated on the neighbouring La Gomera and most keen golfers won't be put off by the short ferry trip.

30 THE PLAYERS GOLF SHOP
CC El Paso, local 8
Las Chafiras
+34 922 736 743
playersgolfshop.com

Forgot to pack your favourite club or that special cap? This is a shop that has specialised in selling a complete array of golf items by the main and most prestigious brands. It is the biggest in its kind on the archipelago, also well-known for renting and repairing golf material.

31 SOUTH TENERIFE GOLF SERVICES
+34 822 680 100
*southtenerifegolf
services.com*

If you're looking for a reliable company to take the hassle out of your golf reservations, this is the largest golf booking agency based in Tenerife. They guarantee golf tee times and cater for singles as well as societies. Other services include club hire, buggy hire and daily transport.

Unusual **ACTIVITIES**

32 FORESTAL PARK

Ctra. TF-24, km 16
Las Lagunetas
+34 630 385 742
forestalparktenerife.es

Offering various open-air circuits with different difficulty levels to choose from, this adventure themed park is perfect for a fun family-outing. Rope ladders and obstacles, Tarzan swings, giant ziplines and climbing walls will give you a very unique experience, high up in the treetops. A challenging outdoor activity in a natural protected area, surrounded by Canarian pine forests.

33 BLOKO DEL VALLE

(various locations)
Casa del Llano 2
La Orotava
+34 630 675 834
+34 629 540 176
blokodelvalle.com

Would you like to beat some drum? Bloko del Valle, a nonprofit musical and sociocultural association operating in various countries, brings cultures and citizens together through percussion. Call them to participate in one of their weekly sessions and let the rhythm of the drums carry you away.

34 ACRO YOGA TENERIFE SUR

C/ Arenas Blancas
Playa de las
Américas

Another nonprofit community initiative uniting people through yoga and physical activity. Anyone can join, there is no fee to pay and no experience is required. Every Sunday, between 3 pm and 21.30 pm the Acro Jam takes place in public, on the grass under the palm trees next to hotel H10 Conquistador.

BIG FIESTAS

35 CARNAVAL

Casa del Carnaval
C/ Aguere 19
Santa Cruz
+34 922 046 020
carnavaldetenerife.
com

Definitely the island's biggest fiesta hereby celebrating what is considered one of the world's most popular carnivals. For more than 10 days, the capital attracts people from all over the globe. The most anticipated event is the election of the Carnival Queen. If you can't join the fun, visit the newly opened Casa del Carnaval museum, giving you a taste of this wonderful madness.

36 NIGHT OF SAN JUAN

June 23rd

In other words the shortest and most magical night of the year, when huge bonfires illuminate almost every neighbourhood of the island. The overwhelming smell of smoke lingers on until the following day. Head for the beaches to enjoy the biggest parties and barbecues and jump over the fire three times to ensure good luck!

37 HARVEST FESTIVALS

Various dates

Called *Romerías* they are the island's most colourful fiestas, honouring the town's patron saint, in order to protect the crops against adverse natural disasters. Traditional clothing, typical carts pulled by oxen, folk music, dance, local food and wine are essential elements. The most popular annual *Romerías* are held in Tegueste (San Marcos), La Laguna (San Benito), Adeje (San Sebastian) and Garachico (San Roque).

Leading **CANARIAN ARTISTS**
and where to see their work

38 ÓSCAR DOMÍNGUEZ
(1906-1957)
AT: **TEA**
Av. de San Sebastián 8 Santa Cruz
+34 922 849 057
teatenerife.com

Definitely one of Tenerife's greatest artists. This surrealist painter whose work sells for huge sums, was born in La Laguna and raised in Tacoronte. He won international fame, exhibited worldwide and rubbed shoulders with other masters like Dalí, Picasso and Miró. His long-life disease later led him to suicide. Admire some of his work at TEA in Santa Cruz.

39 CÉSAR MANRIQUE
(1919-1992)
Various locations

Artistic genius César Manrique was born in Lanzarote, an island completely moulded by his creative influence. Famous for his pioneering ecological vision, he also left his mark on Tenerife. To appreciate some of his significant work, visit Puerto de la Cruz and see Lago Martiánez and the access to Playa Jardín; also look in on Parque Marítimo at Santa Cruz.

40 JOSÉ ABAD
(1942)
Main square Candelaria

A contemporary sculptor born in La Laguna. His monumental work, mostly made of iron, is present at various public spaces in the capital. Above all, he is known for his impressive bronze statues of Tenerife's nine former Guanche kings, called *Menceyes*. Check them out at Candelaria, on the square in front of the basilica.

38   ÓSCAR DOMÍNGUEZ AT TACORONTE

Famous **FACES**

41 **3 OF THE 4 BEATLES**

In 1963, three young boys called Paul McCartney, Ringo Starr and George Harrison, enjoyed their stay on the island but wondered why no one recognised them. They even offered to give a free concert at the Lido Club in Puerto de la Cruz, but were turned down as "it wasn't the place for long-haired rockers"!

42 **U2**

The Irish band U2 visited Tenerife in 1991. Dressed up as women, they happily celebrated Carnaval in the streets of Santa Cruz. At that time they were promoting their album *Achtung Baby*. On the sleeve of the recording you'll find photos of Las Teresitas Beach and the adjoining little cemetery of San Andrés.

43 **STEPHEN HAWKING/ BRIAN MAY**

The late British physicist Stephen Hawking attended the prestigious Starmus Festival, which unites music and astronomy. Celebrated on the island in 2011, 2014 and 2016, another remarkable speaker was Brian May, ex-Queen guitarist and holder of an astronomy degree. He wrote the hit song *Tie your mother down* at Teide Observatory.

Mysterious **HISTORICAL CHARACTERS**

44 **AMARO PARGO**
(1678-1747)
AT: **Santo Domingo**
de Guzmán Church
Plaza Santo
Domingo 7
La Laguna

Born in La Laguna, Amaro Pargo was one of the world's most notorious pirates. Towards the end of his life, through his friendship with Sister María de Jesús, he became a pious citizen and donated large amounts of his fortune to the poor. Part of his treasure remains hidden though and no one has found it... yet! See his tombstone at the Santo Domingo de Guzmán church in La Laguna.

45 **SISTER MARÍA**
DE JESÚS
(1643-1731)
AT: **Santa Catalina**
Monastery
C/ Dean Palahi 1
La Laguna

Pirate Amaro Pargo's confidante, also called *La Siervita*, was known to be an extremely devoted nun. After her death, her corpse has remained mysteriously intact. Each year on February 15th, her remains are exposed to the public at the convent of Santa Catalina in La Laguna. Doors open at 5.30 am for the crowds of people who come to pay respect.

HOLLYWOOD MOVIES
shot in Tenerife

46 **ONE MILLION YEARS B.C.** 1966

A huge Hollywood box-office hit starring Raquel Welch, one of the sexiest woman in cinematic history. In the movie she represents a prehistoric cavewoman wearing mankind's first bikini. A smouldering Mount Teide can be spotted several times, but the plume of smoke was of course optically 'photoshopped' over the summit.

47 **CLASH OF THE TITANS** 2010 / **WRATH OF THE TITANS** 2012

More than 40 years later Hollywood returns with an 80-million-dollar production. Inspired by classic Greek mythology, the movie narrates the odyssey of young Perseus (Sam Worthington), son of Zeus (Liam Neeson), brought up by mortals on earth. The follow-up movie, *Wrath of the Titans*, was also filmed on Tenerife.

48 **FAST & FURIOUS 6** 2013

The sixth instalment of the F&F sequel is a hard-core action movie. Much of the stunt work was done on the motorway between Adeje and Santiago del Teide. Some stretches were even re-paved to make the roads as smooth as a billiard-table top. Huge crowds showed up each day to watch, so check out many of the stunts recorded by locals on YouTube.

49 **BOURNE 5**
2016

The latest super production, filmed mainly in the island's capital, is the fifth Jason Bourne action sequel, starring award-winning Matt Damon. For a few days the streets of Santa Cruz were transformed into the bustling city of Athens, recreating the famous Syntagma Square.

48 **FAST & FURIOUS 6**

1
SANTA CRUZ

In Santa Cruz, like in most capital cities located by the sea or the ocean, there is the additional charm of the water and the port, with its hustle and bustle and its open invitation towards the unknown. This lively city, best known for its colourful Carnaval, has a lot to offer, but back in 1494, when the town was founded, it was only a small fishing village. Historic remains of its distant past are nowadays mingled with modern internationally acclaimed constructions, giving the city its 21st-century appeal.

The area around the harbour is the real heart of the city. All year round a large number of foreign cruise ships dock here, as well as vessels connecting with the eastern Canary Islands and mainland Spain. Besides, Tenerife's strategic position between three different continents explains the port's important commercial activity.

The city itself is a highly friendly place, with a mixture of dynamic streets and lush subtropical parks and squares. Pedestrian shopping streets, markets and vibrant commercial centres help contribute to the busy ambience. Keeping in tune with the real Canarian spirit, a terraced bar or restaurant is never far off, providing a chance to replenish dwindling energy levels with a sweet *barraquito* or a tasty little tapa.

Culture-lovers will take pleasure in several of the capital's top museums, art spaces and street sculptures, whereas foodies will revel at the available choice. And should things get too stressful… there's always Las Teresitas beach to escape to.

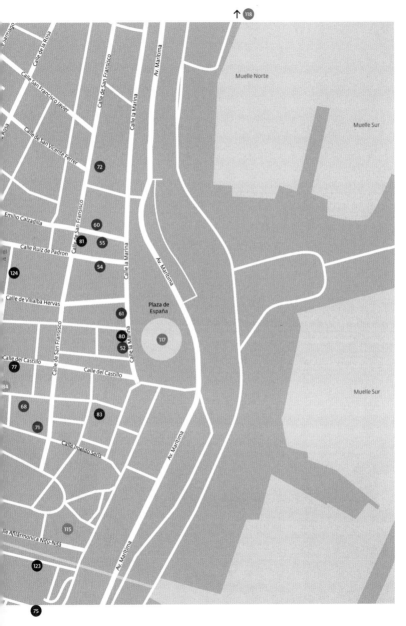

↑ 118

Muelle Norte

Muelle Sur

Muelle Sur

Calle de Santiago
Calle de la Rosa
Calle San Francisco
Calle San Francisco Javier
Av. Marítima
Calle la Marina
Calle de San Vicente Ferrer
72
Emilio Calzadilla
Calle de San Fransisco
60
Calle Ruiz de Padron
81
55
54
Calle la Marina
Av. Marítima
124
Calle de Villalba Hervas
61
Plaza de
España
Calle de San Fransisco
80
117
52
Calle la Marina
Calle del Castillo
77
Calle del Castillo
84
68
83
71
Calle Imeldo Seris
Av. Marítima
115
Calle Afilarmonica Nifú-Nifá
123
75

EAT   —   **DRINK**   —   SHOP   —   BUILDINGS   —   DISCOVER   —   **CULTURE**   —   SLEEP   —   **WEEKEND**   —   RANDOM

AUDITORIO ADÁN MARTÍN

EAT

DRINK

SHOP

BUILDINGS

DISCOVER

CULTURE

SLEEP

Places for **B A G U E T T E** *lovers*

50 **LA GARRIGA**
C/ Pérez Galdós 24
Santa Cruz
+34 922 285 501

There's not a soul in the capital (and far outside its limits) who hasn't waited in a line to buy the unrivalled freshly-made *Bocadillo de Tortilla* (Spanish omelette baguette) at La Garriga's. Operating since 1956 they recently moved to newer and bigger premises. Although the seedy charm of the old place has been lost, the quality of their goods has luckily stayed the same.

51 **DEPATANEGRA**
C/ San Clemente 27
Santa Cruz
+34 630 857 248

This store, of which there is another one in La Orotava, specialises in Iberian ham. You can buy a whole leg of ham that will be cleaned and vacuum packed for you to take back home. If this sounds too much for you, take a seat instead in their cosy corner at the back and savour a juicy *Bocadillo Ibérico* with a nice glass of wine and some excellent cheese.

52 **CAFÉ CARAMBA**
C/ La Marina 1
Santa Cruz
cafecaramba.com

A cutting-edge artisanal sandwich bar specialising in heavily filled and tightly crammed baguettes or sandwiches. Different types of bread are used and together with your choice of drink, soup or salad you can create a perfect lunch. Watch the urban world go by on their outdoor terrace in the very heart of the city.

Feasts for **FOODIES**

53 **CORTXO GASTROBAR**
**Plaza de Ireneo González 5
Santa Cruz
+34 922 151 695**

Walls lined from top to bottom with wine corks, this posh tapa bar has 'creative' stamped all over it. Seating inside is limited but its outdoor terrace, sheltered by the peaceful atmosphere of the Plaza de Ireneo González, is just as nice. Highly frequented for its first-rate standards, added to the fact they don't take reservations, makes it difficult to get hold of a table especially at weekends; so mid-week is probably your best bet.

53 **CORTXO GASTROBAR**

54 KAZAN

**Paseo Milicias
de Garachico 1,
local 4
Santa Cruz
+34 922 245 598**
*restaurantekazan.
com*

The name of this Japanese restaurant translates into 'fire mountain' or volcano. This is not your run-of-the-mill Asian sushi-place, but one of the island's leading restaurants that has been awarded with a Michelin star. The austere zen interior combines well with the perfectly prepared and laid-out dishes, in which only the highest quality ingredients are used.

55 LA BRUJULA

**C/ Emilio
Calzadilla 3
Santa Cruz
+34 822 174 986**

No starched linen, silver cutlery or crystal glasses, but a simple layout and a very friendly atmosphere is what you will find at one of the best and fair-priced restaurants in town. Two Italian relatives have managed to create this little gem specialising in seafood and boasting traditional Italian food at its finest, all prepared with a cheeky twist.

FOREIGN EATS

56 CONVIVIO

C/ Numancia 19
Santa Cruz
+34 922 152 613

A morning stroll through Parque García Sanabria combines perfectly well with lunch at this popular and artisanal Italian little eatery situated opposite the park. Their strong points are tasty fried *Napolitano* pizza (also gluten-free options) and fresh semolina flour pasta. A pleasant detail while you are waiting is the small glass of cava on the house.

57 EL LÍBANO

C/ de Santiago
Cuadrado 36
Santa Cruz
+34 922 285 914
*restauranteellibano.
com*

At El Líbano they serve authentic Lebanese food and they have been doing so for the past 35 years. The somewhat middle-eastern setting dotted with a few shisha pipes is maybe a bit outdated; on the other hand, the food and the prices keep the many regulars returning to this beloved place. Don't leave without tasting the sweetest pastries filled to the brim with pistachios, walnuts and honey.

58 DARESHASU

C/ Suarez Guerra 47
Santa Cruz
+34 822 042 725
*cemtenerife.es/
dareshasu*

Vegan friendly, Japanese and Filipino are the common denominators to classify this little jewel in the centre of the city. As it is a long, small and narrow restaurant there are only a few tables to sit at, so remember to book in advance or alternatively consider ordering a takeaway. With its nice staff and its rich choice of excellent dishes, everyone simply loves Dareshasu.

ICE CREAM *and* CREPES

59 **MIO GELATO**
C/ El Pilar 8
Santa Cruz
+34 922 271 055
miogelato.es

If you like ice cream, this big and bright-coloured place is heaven. There are over 100 flavours to choose from; or you can be creative and combine your ice cream with fresh fruit, biscuits and candy. They also prepare velvety milk shakes and natural yogurt, made with milk from north Tenerife and served with a topping of your choice.

60 **LA BOHEME**
C/ Emilio
Calzadilla 8
Santa Cruz
+34 922 296 296
creperialaboheme.es

With more than 15 years of experience this crepe-restaurant has become an institution amongst the *chicharreros* (nickname for people born in the capital). Sweet or savoury (meat, fish or veggie), you can create your own personalised crepe or simply enjoy one of their healthy salads named after places on the Canary Islands.

61 **EL DULCE ANGOLO DE ROSITAS**
La Marina 3
Santa Cruz
+34 602 648 948

This little Italian ice-cream parlour, right next to Plaza de España, with its lollipop interior and its friendly young girls serving you with a smile, deserves to be mentioned as a place to savour an excellent Italian coffee together with a real artisanal and smooth ice cream, of the kind you get served in the south of Italy.

62 **HELADOS CALIFORNIA**
Various locations

The antique red, blue and white California ice-cream vans, driving around the streets to the sound of Lili Marlene, have been selling their delicious strawberry and cream flavoured ice creams to each person young and old for the past 50 years. Watch out for this icon if you don't want to miss one of the most beloved traditions on the island.

GO LOCAL
– popular places chicharreros love

---

63 TASCA LA MONTERÍA
Callejón del Combate 12
Santa Cruz
+34 698 504 456
+34 822 258 387

Tasca La Montería has been awarded for serving the best tapas at the 'Ruta de la Tapa' contest within the commercial Soho zone. It is the perfect place for a good lunch or a menu-of-the-day offer. A few of the favourites are mushrooms filled with Serrano ham, or pork with onion jam and cinnamon on toast.

64 PANZABURRO GASTROTASCA
C/ Mendez Núñez 20
Santa Cruz
+34 674 962 041
panzaburro.info

Situated in the heart of the city and known as one of the best gastronomic proposals in the capital, this ecological restaurant gets its fresh organic flavours out of its own garden located high up in the mountains of Anaga. Very innovative, with every dish looking like a little piece of art, this place has a great atmosphere and a good service.

65 CUC – COCINA URBANA CANARIA
Prolongación de Ramón y Cajal 5
Santa Cruz
+34 922 892 264

Popular chef Nacho Solano, together with his sommelier wife Erika Sanz, are behind this fresh concept, sinking into the roots of the tasty Canarian cuisine, but reinterpreting it in a fun way. If you are a wine-lover try a glass of their phenomenal 'Suertes del Marqués' (*suertesdelmarques.com*) to accompany a plate of their Old Ropa *(Ropa Vieja)*, an all-time favourite in every Canarian household.

66 COCINA URBANA

Rambla de Santa Cruz 114
Santa Cruz
+34 822 026 677

Cocina Urbana shouldn't be confused with the above mentioned restaurant. This cosy venue with its contemporary interior is mainly popular for its exquisite Urban Hamburgers (veggie option available). A good selection of local wines and more than excellent coffees, together with an after-dinner stroll on La Rambla, make this little place an urban favourite.

67 EL PORRÓN TASCA ANDALUZA

C/ Antonio Domínguez Alfonso 36
Santa Cruz
+34 922 151 867
el-porron.business. site

This tapas bar is located in La Noria, which is one of the oldest neighbourhoods in Santa Cruz and an area famous for its many outstanding little restaurants and bars. El Porrón is a tiny place with minimum outdoor seating so you might end up sitting at the bar. They serve Andalusian as well as Canarian tapas that have been spiced up to be anything but boring. The waiters will happily assist you if you are not sure what to choose.

64　PANZABURRO GASTROTASCA

Very **TRADITIONAL**

68 LA HIERBITA
C/ El Clavel 19
Santa Cruz
+34 922 244 617
lahierbita.com

Around the corner of Teatro Guimerá, the oldest theatre of the Canary Islands, this ancient restaurant has been operative since 1893. It was the first eatery in town to receive a business license. The double-storey mansion has maintained its original structure and the decoration with antique and traditional objects of the island is very authentic. It's a popular urban place to try local food, in a pure Canarian setting.

69 GUACHINCHE LA CUEVA DE CASIANO
C/ Chafira 58 (Las Moraditas de Taco)
Santa Cruz
+34 666 369 814
guachinche-la-cueva-de-casiano.webnode.es

Situated inside a cave(!) on the outskirts of town, between Santa Cruz and La Laguna. Come here with a big appetite, wanting to experience the real deal. No frills, but only homemade hearty food, the same as ever, served in an animated environment with *Tinerfeños* often singing along to their traditional music and eating their beloved food. Favourites are: Casiano's sweet potato salad and *Secreto Ibérico*.

70 BODEGÓN EL PUNTERO

C/ San Clemente 5
Santa Cruz
+34 922 282 214

Another long-established place to try out the classical loved-by-the-locals Canarian food is at El Puntero, where they only serve fish and local wine. There is no menu, no coffee and the very humble, authentic venue takes you back to gone-by days. Give it a try and like all real *chicharreros*, you will surely be back for more.

71 BODEGUITA CANARIA

C/ Imeldo Seris 18
Santa Cruz
+34 922 293 216
*bodeguitacanaria.
com*

Bodeguita Canaria, founded in 1999, has been awarded several times for its authentic gastronomy. They serve typical dishes that have been passed on from generation to generation, never revealing the fine secrets of their elaboration. Located very centrally, near the Plaza de España, the decoration has been kept accordingly: very familiar, simple and traditional.

You are what you – **N O M E A T** – *eat*

---

72 KIMPIRA
C/ de San Vicente
Ferrer 5, Plaza
Isabel II
Santa Cruz
+34 922 242 606

Since 1995 this macrobiotic restaurant has been looking after the city's non-meat eaters in a responsible way. Their daily menus, consisting of 3 courses, are well-balanced and offer a nutritious gastronomy. Kimpira is opened during lunch hours only. The name of the restaurant refers to a Japanese cooking style of 'sauté and simmer'.

73 VÍA ORGÁNICA
C/ San Clemente
39, local 4
Santa Cruz
+34 822 179 157
via-organica.es

Come here to taste original food prepared with a philosophy: only local ecological products assuring maximum freshness; nothing but wholemeal flour and cereals contributing to a better health; no refined sugars and low temperature cooking. They serve dishes full of goodness for all lovers of clean and healthy food, but also diabetics and those with allergies or coeliac disease are well-attended. Vegan cooking courses are available.

73 · VÍA ORGÁNICA

COFFEE, TEA *and* CAKES

74 LA CASITA

C/ Jesús Nazareno
14
Santa Cruz
+34 922 247 851

The two-storey 'Little House' was opened in 2011 by Nuria and Naira, who covered the walls of this cute little venue, which opens up to a mini upper-terrace, with old pictures of their families. You'll find sweet and savoury in the form of succulent 100% beef homemade burgers and finger-licking cakes, of which their Banoffee and Red Velvet are simply irresistible.

75 EL CORTE INGLÉS

Av. Tres de Mayo 7
Santa Cruz
+34 922 849 400
restauracion.
elcorteingles.es

This multi-storey building has impressive views of the Santa Cruz harbour and its famous opera house. After shopping at what is considered the most classy Spanish chain of department stores, take a break at the bakery and cafe on the ground floor or go to the upper level, where you will find the restaurant area with more coffee and cakes on offer.

76 LA PAJARITA

C/ de Cairasco 13
Santa Cruz
+34 608 403 639

You will find a healthy natural alternative to your ordinary bakery at La Pajarita. They not only sell and serve eco-vegan cakes, muffins, ice cream and cookies, but also a range of other ecological products such as sandwiches and toasts, buddha bowls, freshly squeezed juices or shakes and the best Frappuccino in town.

77 PALMELITA

C/ Castillo 9
Santa Cruz
+34 922 888 904
palmelita.es

Don't miss this beautiful old-style bakery on the corner of Calle Castillo, the capital's longest and most famous pedestrian shopping street. Sit outside to watch the world go by or take a high seat at the bar to enjoy a well-made *barraquito* coffee and a slice of one of their yummy creamy cakes. An all-time favourite with locals.

77 PALMELITA

MYTHICAL BARS *and* JUICE BARS

---

78 VIVA MARÍA
C/ Suarez Guerra
20
Santa Cruz
+34 922 273 061

Operative since 1979, Viva María's bright interior is in tune with the wide array of fresh natural juices on offer. Sit at the busy bar to see them blend the juice you chose from their list or the one you created yourself by mixing the fruit you love most. Add a healthy sandwich and your vitamin level will be restored, allowing you to continue your day.

79 DOÑA PAPAYA
C/ de Callao de
Lima 3
Santa Cruz
+34 922 290 679

Apart from all the different kinds of juices to be savoured at this popular *zumería*, special attention should be given to their famous *Doña Papaya* milk shake made with papaya, almonds and *merengada* milk (a Spanish recipe the main ingredients of which are milk, sugar, egg white and cinnamon). A must-try.

80 CAFÉ ATLÁNTICO
C/ La Marina 1
Santa Cruz
+34 922 246 909

Having risen to its status of city-icon after more than 70 years of history, this stylish bar with its unique interior, its grand terrace and its magnificent location between the Plaza de España and the Plaza de Candelaria attracts many locals and tourists at all hours of the daytime. In the evenings it's a favourite meeting point before hitting the town and at weekends it tends to get extra busy with regular events taking place.

EVENING *and* NIGHTTIME TERRACES

81 WINE & CHEESE BAR

C/ de San Francisco 28
Santa Cruz
+34 654 132 558

The narrow and sloping San Francisco square with its huge centenarian rubber trees has an undeniable charm. The square takes its name from the beautiful baroque church built in 1680. This whole quarter has become a pleasant area for having a few evening drinks while listening to good music. The warm smell of maturing cheese is what will attract you to the Wine & Cheese Bar, where you can ask the sommelier to advise you on any of their nice combinations.

82 BULAN

C/ Antonio Dominguez Alfonso 35
Santa Cruz
+34 922 274 116
bulantenerife.com

To the side of the Conception Church, Santa Cruz's oldest church, which contains *The Cross* carried by the conqueror Fernández de Lugo, is Antonio Dominguez Alfonso Street. Still called La Noria by locals, this is a historic area where many carnival groups have their headquarters. At nighttime this quiet pedestrian street turns into one of the busiest streets with several excellent bars.

83 EL ÁTICO BY NH

C/ Candelaria 3
Santa Cruz
+34 634 700 027

This city-view rooftop terrace belonging to the NH Hotel, is the ultimate open-air urban chill-out club, open from 5 pm till 3 am (check for changing summer and winter opening times). You can either make an appearance for an early-evening coffee or arrive with friends for a late-night drink and dance, while watching the beau monde of Santa Cruz.

81 WINE & CHEESE BAR

SECONDHAND

stores and markets

84 KISH VINTAGE APPAREL

C/ Doctor Allart 32
Santa Cruz
+34 922 196 045

If you are looking for a blast from the past that is still able to pack a fashion punch, then look no further than this little vintage and used-clothing store attracting a hipster clientele. They also offer a nice selection of gift objects with a fairly recent history.

85 MAITE ANTIGÜEDADES

C/ Santa Rosalía 32
Santa Cruz
+34 922 246 118

Maite's antique and gift shop is located in the centre of Santa Cruz. Come here to find fine antique furniture, a carefully selected and high-quality range of European and British porcelain items, silverware, crystal, wooden boxes, clocks, jewellery and whatever else that has caught the owner's fancy.

86 FLAMINGOS VINTAGE KILO

C/ Sabino
Berthelot 3
Santa Cruz
+34 610 775 432
vintagekilo.com

There are 24 stores in Spain belonging to this franchise that sells vintage and secondhand American clothes by the kilo, both for him and for her. Here are a few typical examples of what you will encounter: colourful Hawaiian shirts, blue jeans and denim dungarees, All Star sneakers and American football strips. A fun store worth a visit.

87 **RASTRO DE SANTA CRUZ**

Av. José Manuel
Guimerá
Santa Cruz
+34 922 279 941

Held every Sunday morning from 8 am till 2 pm, this is the largest and most famous flea market on the island with traders selling a nice mixture of old and new bric-a-brac, clothing and antiques. The Rastro has become an unmissable event for a lazy Sunday stroll and its familiar relaxed atmosphere attracts many people from all over Tenerife.

88 MERCADO NUESTRA SEÑORA DE ÁFRICA 'LA RECOVA'

Buying **GOURMET**
among other things

88 **MERCADO NUESTRA SEÑORA DE ÁFRICA 'LA RECOVA'**

Av. de San Sebastián 51
Santa Cruz
la-recova.com

This must-see colourful and lively market, also called *La Recova*, is part of the capital's living history. Opened in 1944, it's the place where residents come for their fruit and veg, fish and meat, and also buy fresh-cut flowers and plants. Most stalls are arranged around an open central patio, but there's also a lower floor where fish and seafood are sold (and eaten). Take a stroll to locate the Canarian gourmet food on offer, or have a coffee and a bite at the cafeteria.

89 **ESPACIO DEL GOURMET**

Av. Bravo Murillo 16
Santa Cruz
+34 922 535 535
espaciodelgourmet. com

Espacio del Gourmet specialises in the best Canarian products and the finest national and international aliments. Whether you are looking for fine wines or cheeses, jams or marmalades, foie gras or pâtés, Belgian chocolates, champagne, caviar or even exceptional oils and vinegars, this is the place to find them. Also famous for their first-class gift hampers.

S U R F *and* **S K A T E** *shops*

90 **KORNER STREET**
C/ Bethencourt
Alfonso 35
Santa Cruz
+34 822 179 189
kornerst.com

If you are not sure which board to buy, let the friendly staff guide you to help you choose your skateboard within the range of street-skates, cruiser or downhill long-skates and surf-skates. Apart from trucks and wheels you will also find skate and streetwear clothing and shoes from leading brands.

91 **MIDWAY SURF STUFF**
C/ Pérez Galdos 12
Santa Cruz
+34 922 534 135

This small neon-lit corner store crammed with different types of skate and surf boards, also offers many original and appropriate accessories, sneakers and clothing, amongst which some very cute Star Wars socks definitely caught our fancy.

92 **AJ PROJECT**
C/ Robayna 5
Santa Cruz
+34 922 574 152
ajprojectskate.com

Should you have an unusual large shoesize (48/49), then check out the large selection of good quality sneakers and sports shoes in all shapes and sizes, even if you are looking for limited editions within the premier brands. Also pay them a visit for their creative skate clothing and accessories.

93 **AS17 SHOP**
C/ Teobaldo
Power 24
Santa Cruz
+34 685 932 828

This store is named after Acosta Silvia, the adolescent founder of the shop, offering a wide range of very technical surf and bodyboard products. She also sells surf textile, sunglasses and accessories. In addition she provides a repair service for surf boards as well as a sales service for secondhand boards.

91 **MIDWAY SURF STUFF**

BOOKS, COMICS
and MUSIC

94 LIBRERÍA CANARY BOOKS

C/ Porlier 79
Santa Cruz
+34 922 271 715
canarybooks.net

Librería Canary Books has been the island's number one bookshop in foreign languages for the last 30 years. Although they specialise in language text books for students of all ages and levels, they also have a fairly good selection of English and German novels, plus a number of French titles to choose from.

95 COMICS Y MAZMORRAS

C/ Ramón y Cajal 11
Santa Cruz
+34 922 029 926
comicsymaz morras.blogspot.be

All comic geeks and freaks will find this place a treat. Whether it's just a comic you're after or the latest miniature figurines, alternative board and role-playing games of the kind no other store sells, or even your favourite Pokémon T-shirt, it's all here. A store that will understand your special needs.

96 BLOUS AND MUSIC

C/ Bethencourt
Alfonso 34
Santa Cruz
+34 922 270 889

With a second branch in La Laguna, this is one of the few places that sells vinyl records and record-players. The stock is focussed on the myths and classics of music history and cinema; not only in vinyl, but also in DVD, Blu Ray, posters, T-shirts and merchandise.

Helping you get
THE ISLAND LOOK

97 PAMPLING

C/ Castillo 63,
local 1
Santa Cruz
+34 922 089 266
pampling.com

Living in a warm climate, a personalised T-shirt is an essential element of your wardrobe and your appearance. At Pampling you can either enter the ongoing competition for the most original design with your own personal design, or you can simply buy one of the many existing T-shirts by designers from all over the world.

98 MAMIHLAPI-NATAPAI

C/ Teobaldo
Power 17
Santa Cruz
+34 922 151 337

The name of this boutique (known as the world's most concise word) is part of the vocabulary of the *Yámanas* Indians in the Land of Fire. It's a shop that focusses on alternative women's T-shirts and jewellery compliments brought back from different corners of the globe.

99 GLORY SUNGLASS

CC Castillo, local 10
C/ Imeldo Serís 64
Santa Cruz
+34 922 243 052

Another unmistakable item that is part of the island look is a nice pair of sunglasses. At Glory you will encounter a large variety of the latest models at very modest prices. If you are looking for something different and unique to complete your image, pay them a visit; you won't be disappointed.

100 SIN RENCOR TATTOO

C/ San Lucas 14
Santa Cruz
+34 922 296 014

The finishing touch is a colourful tattoo, no doubt about it. With the good fortune of not having to hide under layers and layers of clothing for most parts of the year, there are quite a few good tattoo parlours in Santa Cruz. Pachu is the main artist at Sin Rencor and his successful use of bright colours makes him one of the favourites.

Classy **FASHION SHOPS**
for him and for her

101 **HUTTON**

C/ Suarez Guerra 38
Santa Cruz
+34 822 665 967
hutton.es

With three stores in Madrid, one in Alicante and another in Gran Canaria, this classic men's store imposes the typical British style upon the capital. It has become a favourite for those wanting to dress in an elegant manner. In spite of the English name, this label with its cute little taxi emblem, is 100% Spanish and is ideal for shirts, blazers, polos, nice ties, socks and underwear.

102 **EL GANSO**

C/ del Castillo 19
Santa Cruz
+34 822 175 734
elganso.com

This men's fashion company, also represented in the luxurious Corte Inglés department store, has its own shop in the emblematic pedestrian street Calle del Castillo, the commercial heart of the city. A nice mix of vanguard with a European cosmopolitan air and some very Spanish influences make this a funky shop. Their elegant sneakers are basics in any man's wardrobe.

103 **SILBÓN**

C/ Suarez
Guerra 40
Santa Cruz
+34 922 287 153
silbon.es

Think Paul Newman or Robert Redford and you will have an idea of what sells in this men's fashion store. Known for their classy style, their offer includes Casual Wear, The City and Tailoring. If you don't want to take any risks, Silbón will always be your surest bet.

104 **BOUNTY**

C/ el Pilar 40
Santa Cruz
+34 922 288 211
bountycanarias.com

In 1980 the tiny Bounty men's boutique started up in Puerto de la Cruz and quickly grew out to become a quality chain with more than 14 retail outlets. They have always specialised in high-end fashion, which now also includes female couture with brands like Valentino, Kenzo, Jimmy Choo, Prada and others.

105 **KOL-MAN**

C/ el Pilar 25
Santa Cruz
+34 922 271 917
kolman.es

This high-end boutique, part of a third generation family business (their grandfather was one of the capital's first tailors), offers a beautiful range for women seeking modern classics and a high level of quality brand-led clothing, shoes, bags, jewellery and sunglasses. Their outlet zone usually presents great bargains.

Exceptional **GIFT SHOPS**

106 **DE CURBELO**
C/ San Clemente 8
Santa Cruz
+34 922 534 621

You will probably find Salvador de Curbelo, artist and owner of this shop, at his old Singer machine, stitching one of his unique leather bags. Salva only sells distinctive objects either made by himself or other famous Spanish artisans like Javier Sánchez Medina, Patricia Delgado or Nuria Blanco. The singular shoe-lasts that decorate the interior of his atelier belonged to his father and are unfortunately not for sale. Come here if you are looking for something different.

107 **TIENDA TEA**
Av. de San
Sebastián 8
Santa Cruz
+34 922 849 070
teatenerife.es

Every great museum normally has a nice museum shop. Don't expect anything less at TEA (Tenerife Espacio de Arte). The boutique at the entrance of the building is not only a place to look for glossy art books, but it also offers unique jewellery, textile and handicraft creations by the leading local artisans and designers. A great gift shop to buy an exclusive present for someone special.

SHOPS *for* KIDS

108 LA ORMIGA

C/ Teobaldo Power 30
Santa Cruz
+34 822 176 997
laormiga.com

If there's that marked occasion when you want your kids dressed like little princes and princesses, La Ormiga is a must. This small 30-square-metre shop is one of the cutest places to buy elegant fashion for your children up to the age of 16. Their clothes are comfortable, colourful and made in Spain.

109 CALZADOS EL ZAPATITO

C/ Imeldo Seris 48
Santa Cruz
+34 822 258 838

The perfect frock requires an equally perfect matched pair of shoes. Decent and good-quality children's footwear for all types of occasions, that is what you will find at El Zapatito. They specialise in baby shoes and sell up to size 43 in school moccasins.

110 LA NIÑA

C/ Viera y Clavijo 1
Santa Cruz
+34 922 287 989

You will have a hard time pulling yourself and your children away from this dainty novelty store filled with plenty of curious and enticing little objects: unicorn pens that light up, origami books, glow-in-the-dark snow globes, cute miniature dollies, original stationery and many more fascinating gadgets.

MODERN
ARCHITECTURAL *jewels*

111 AUDITORIO ADÁN MARTÍN

Av. de la
Constitución 1
Santa Cruz
+34 922 568 600
*auditoriodetenerife.
com*

The shiny-white auditorium, resembling a giant boat anchored at the waterfront, is the work of acclaimed architect Santiago Calatrava. It is a stunning building with strong sculptural impact that has two big concert halls, seating respectively 1658 and 428 people. Check out their agenda for cultural events or visit on a guided tour.

112 TEA – TENERIFE ESPACIO DE LAS ARTES

Av. de San
Sebastián 8
Santa Cruz
+34 922 849 060
teatenerife.es

This building by Herzog & de Meuron, along with the Calatrava Auditorium, has changed the image of Santa Cruz. Its austere concrete façade has over 1200 openings in 720 different shapes, creating a surprising nightly image. The geometrically shaped construction comprises a public library, a contemporary art museum, a boutique, a cafeteria, the Photography Centre of the island and several spaces for public use.

113 ESCUELA DE ARTES ESCÉNICAS

C/ Pedro Suárez
Hernández
Santa Cruz
+34 922 220 204
webeac.org

The School of Dramatic Arts presents itself as a huge stage platform against the backdrop of the city and its natural surroundings. This avant-garde project using concrete, glass, wood and a zig-zag ramp was designed by GPY Architectos and is situated in the upper part of town.

112 **TEA – TENERIFE ESPACIO DE LAS ARTES**

The best **TRADITIONAL ARCHITECTURE**

114 **TEATRO GUIMERÁ**

Plaza Isla de la
Madera 2
Santa Cruz
+34 922 609 409
teatroguimera.es

Inaugurated in 1851, the beautiful Guimerá Theatre is the oldest theatre on the Canary Islands. It is named after writer, poet and dramaturg Angel Guimerá who was born in Santa Cruz. The building is in romantic classicist style, but its interior has been completely reformed. The sculpture of a face located in front of the theatre is by Polish artist Igor Mitoraj.

114 **TEATRO GUIMERÁ**

115 IGLESIA DE NUESTRA SEÑORA DE LA CONCEPCIÓN

Plaza de la Iglesia 2
Santa Cruz
+34 922 242 384

This church, as well as being one of the oldest catholic temples within the religious architecture of the Canary Islands, is the most important and recognisable one of the capital. It stands out as the only church of the archipelago consisting of five naves and its imposing tower presides the old historic town (La Noria). Noteworthy are the Canarian balconies on its main façade.

116 MASONIC TEMPLE

C/ de San Lucas 35
Santa Cruz
*templomasonico
tenerife.es*

Men sphinxes guard the temple and the Eye of Providence is to be seen in the upper fronton. These and many more masonic symbols can be contemplated at this fantastic neoclassical building, inaugurated in 1904 and declared an Asset of Cultural Interest in 2007. Sadly in disuse, the building is waiting to be rehabilitated and converted into a Centre of Interpretation for Freemasonry.

NOT TO MISS

117 PLAZA DE ESPAÑA

Centro de
Interpretación
'Castillo de San
Cristóbal'
Av. Marítima 128
Santa Cruz
+34 922 285 605
museosdetenerife.org

Completely remodelled by Herzog & de Meuron, this is the largest plaza on the Canary Islands. The new square, inaugurated in 2008, contains a huge saltwater lake and a fountain jet. During the works, old remains of Tenerife's historic defence system were excavated and incorporated into the project by means of a free museum situated below the square. Here you will also see the legendary canon El Tigre, which tore off Admiral Nelson's arm when he tried to conquer the island in 1797.

117 PLAZA DE ESPAÑA

118 LAS TERESITAS BEACH

Av. Marítima de
San Andrés
Santa Cruz

This idyllic urban beach, covered with fine Sahara-imported sand, dotted with exotic palm trees and set against the fairy-tale landscape of the Anaga mountains, is a must-see. The concrete breakwaters, protecting against strong currents and waves, make it an ideal family beach. Additional assets are: a large parking zone, complete facilities, the Cofradía de Pescadores where you can savour a fresh fish lunch and the vicinity of the authentic little fishing village San Andrés.

119 LA RAMBLA

Santa Cruz

La Rambla is the capital's artery, crossing the city from one end to the other. A boulevard lined with beautiful palm trees, huge Indian laurels, colourful flamboyants and jacarandas, fresh flowers, amazing sculptures, benches, kiosks, playgrounds and a pedestrian walkway running down the middle, make it the perfect area for an urban saunter.

PARKS & WALKS

120 PALMETUM
Av. de la
Constitución 5
Santa Cruz
+34 922 229 368
palmetumtenerife.es

What once used to be the city's rubbish dump has now been converted into a unique botanical garden specialising in different kinds of palm trees from all over the world. Palmetum not only boasts a spectacular vegetation, but also offers some breathtaking vistas of the sea, the city and the Anaga mountains.

121 PARQUE GARCÍA SANABRIA
C/ Méndez
Nuñez 60
Santa Cruz
+34 922 606 099

This public park is a lush botanical garden in which to relax and have a bite, as well as an outdoor art gallery with numerous sculptures. The pretty centrepiece near the entrance is a statue of a voluptuous lady, which the locals refer to as *La Tetona* (the big-breasted woman). Also check out the grand but delicate floral clock, a present from the Danish Consul in 1938.

122 HISTORIC SANTA CRUZ
(guided walks)
Buy tickets at:
Kiosk City Expert
C/ del Castillo
Santa Cruz
+34 922 289 536
cityexpert.es

Every day at noon, with starting point at the Plaza de España, an official guide will take you on an interesting and informative walking tour through the historic part of town in either English or German and Spanish. The tour lasts one hour and costs 2 euro for residents and 5 euro for visitors.

121 **PARQUE GARCÍA SANABRIA**

Miscellaneous
MUSEUMS

123 **MUSEO DE LA NATURALEZA Y EL HOMBRE**
C/ Fuentes Morales
Santa Cruz
+34 922 535 816
museosdetenerife.org

Regarded as the most important museum of Macaronesia, its fame is mainly due to its formidable collection of Guanche mummies and its reputation of being a world reference in regard to their preservation. Expect a precise and entertaining display of the natural riches of the islands, including reptiles, birds and bugs, and of the pre-Hispanic people that populated the territory.

124 **MUSEO DE BELLAS ARTES**
C/ Jose Murphy 12
Santa Cruz
+34 922 609 446
santacruzmas.com

Founded in 1899, the Museum of Fine Arts has played a pioneering role in the cultural development of the city. Its façade showcases ten busts of local intellectuals and philosophers. The museum's most famous work is the *Tríptico de Nava y Grimón* (by the Flemish Primitives), but most interesting are the pre-arranged guided visits to their storerooms, giving you an unexpected insight into the life and history of the island.

125 CASA DEL CARNAVAL

C/ Aguere 19
Santa Cruz
+34 922 046 020
carnavaldetenerife.com

The recently inaugurated Carnival House is a museum dedicated to the history of this emblematic festival. It is not only an exhibition on what is considered to be one of the best carnivals in the world, but it's also an interactive learning centre and a delight for the senses, the visitors being able to dress up, feel, hear and experience the atmosphere of Santa Cruz's biggest fiesta.

126 FUNDACIÓN CAJA CANARIAS

Plaza del
Patriotismo 1
Santa Cruz
+34 922 471 100
cajacanarias.com

Caja Canarias, which used to be a general savings fund, is now a foundation contributing to the preservation of the Canarian historic-artistic heritage. They offer a constant programme of highly qualitative exhibitions and cultural events. Some of the best exhibitions that have been brought to the island have been seen at their venues. Generally free admission.

Modern ART GALLERIES

127 CÍRCULO DE BELLAS ARTES

C/ del Castillo 43
Santa Cruz
+34 922 246 496
circulobellasartestf. com

Círculo de Bellas Artes was created in 1926 and newly inaugurated in 2016 after architect Fernando Menis renovated the centre. The highlight of Menis' intervention is the original custom-made welcome desk. Also notable is the mural dominating the theatre of the venue as well as the colourful façade of the building, painted by a street artist.
An interesting cultural centre not to be missed.

128 CENTRO DE ARTE LA RECOVA

Plaza Isla de la Madera
Santa Cruz
+34 922 609 412
santacruzmas.com

Located in a beautiful building by Manuel de Oraá dating 1851 and formerly used as the city's market premises, La Recova provides display space for contemporary Canarian and Spanish artists' exhibitions of all kinds. Hosting approximately 12 expositions a year, their International Comic Exhibition has gained a lot of prestige. Free entry.

129 TEA AND CENTRO DE FOTOGRAFÍA

Av. de San Sebastián 8
Santa Cruz
+34 922 849 071
teatenerife.es
fotonoviembre.org

This should be any lover of contemporary art's first stop when visiting the city. Considered one of the best small museums in Spain, TEA is a dynamic centre with a permanent collection focussed on Oscar Domínguez, one of Spain's leading surrealist artists. The gallery also organises temporary exhibitions as well as film screenings and other cultural events. Watch out for the two-yearly international festival called Fotonoviembre, which had its first edition in 1991.

129 TEA AND CENTRO DE FOTOGRAFÍA

STREET ART *old and new*

130 **MURALS**
Santa Cruz
tenerifestreetart.org

In the street artist's words: "A revolution is taking place, moving art out of the museums and into the streets". A great job has certainly been done here by mapping out the nicest street art on the island. All you'll need is your cell phone and the given link and you can take a tag tour to start exploring.

130 **MURALS**

131 LA RAMBLA
I EXPOSICIÓN
INTERNACIONAL DE
ESCULTURA EN LA CALLE
Santa Cruz

In 1973 Santa Cruz hosted the first International Exhibition of Street Sculptures with La Rambla as the main stage. Many artists later donated their work, thus enriching the artistic heritage of the city. Take a stroll along la Rambla and Parque García Sanabria and see exclusive sculptures by Miró, Henry Moore, Martín Chirino, Óscar Domínguez and many others.

132 DÍA DE LA CRUZ
Santa Cruz

Every May 3rd, on the Day of The Cross and in remembrance of the founding of the city in 1494, the capital is brightened up with countless crosses embellished with the most colourful flowers. Adorned by associations and neighbourhoods, the compositions are then awarded for their beauty. This fiesta is also popular in Puerto de la Cruz and in Los Realejos.

Fabulous **FESTIVALS**

---

133 **FESTIVAL INTERNACIONAL DE MÚSICA DE CANARIAS**

C/ Pta Canseco 49, 2°
Santa Cruz
+34 922 531 835
festivaldecanarias.
com

On to its 34th edition in 2018, this grand classical music festival is celebrated in different venues on various islands. In Tenerife the spectacular programme, including internationally renowned artists, takes place in the Adán Martín Auditorium during the months of January and February, which makes it the only European classical music festival held in winter.

134 **CARNAVAL**

Santa Cruz
carnavaldetenerife.
com

Thousands of *Tinerfeños* wait impatiently each year to celebrate their biggest, most colourful and utterly amusing street fiesta called Carnaval. Highlights are: the election of the Queen with dresses up to three metres high and weighing over 100 kilos, the Tuesday Parade where it all comes together, and the burying of the Sardine with the many Wailing Widows saying goodbye to 10 days of madness…

135 **PLENILUNIO**

Santa Cruz
pleniluniosantacruz.
com

Normally twice a year this leisure initiative organises around 100 activities scattered all over town, aimed at children, adults and visitors alike. Food trucks and gastro markets, games and workshops, musical acts, old-timer cars, night races, handicraft markets and many other fun things to do, make this a date to keep in your agenda.

Great **SLEEPS**

136 **HOTEL MENCEY**

C/ Doctor José
Naveiras 38
Santa Cruz
+34 922 609 900
grandhotelmencey.
com

Opened in 1950, the Mencey Hotel is one of the city's symbols. It's an elegant, glamourous and distinguished hotel where most celebrities who have come to the island, have stayed for the night. Located near La Rambla, it has a spa, top-notch dining, indoor as well as outdoor pools, and extreme comfort.

137 **HOTEL ESCUELA**

Av. San Sebastián
152
Santa Cruz
+34 922 847 500
hotelescuela
santacruz.com

More of a business hotel than tourist lodgings, this suits some people better than others. Rooms are very spacious and there's a modern feel to the place. Its location close to the football stadium allows you to move comfortably around the city without the real need of a car or public transport.

138 **B&B DOROTEA**

C/ de Jesús y
María 40
Santa Cruz
+34 651 420 835

This colourful Bed & Breakfast, consisting of five rooms and owned by the Italian couple Luca and Dorotea, couldn't be better situated: it's in the middle of the downtown area. Guests are made to feel very welcome. Good beds, quaint clean rooms, a friendly service and a nice breakfast make this place a favourite with many visitors.

136 **HOTEL MENCEY**

2
THE NORTH

If the South is a place of diversion, deep suntans and Dorada Pilsen, the North has to be experienced in a completely different manner. This is where you run into the authentic Tenerife, where you savour the most typical local food and wines, enjoy the island's historical cultural heritage and become familiar with the green and lush natural areas tucked away in the distant Anaga mountains. Hiking in the upper North is sheer delight, but remember there's always a reason behind a leafy abundant vegetation…

Amongst the must-sees La Laguna, with its history of more than 5 centuries, is top of the list. As the former capital and the place where the Spanish conqueror settled, it was declared a UNESCO World Heritage Site, representing the first example of a grid-plan town. Another urban area with lots of character and traditions is the elegant Villa de la Orotava boasting cobbled streets, old manor houses, beautiful churches and colourful plazas. A tour of the island should also include the quaint Garachico, home to the first harbour on the island but later destroyed by a volcanic eruption, and the nearby town of Icod de los Vinos, known for its iconic dragon tree. Don't miss Puerto de la Cruz, the former stronghold of tourism and nowadays filled with urban art and foodie restaurants in the old fishing neighbourhood of La Ranilla.

And last but not least, go for a rather different dining experience at an authentic *guachinche* (gwah-chin-cheh), where wine from their proper vineyard is served… ¡Salud!

Buenavista
del Norte

La Tierra
del Trigo

Icod de
los Vinos

San Juan de la
Rambla

Pu
la

Garachico

Los Realejos

Los Silos

La Guancha

El Palmar

San Juan
del Reparo

Teno Rural Park

Masca

San José
de los Llanos

Las Portelas

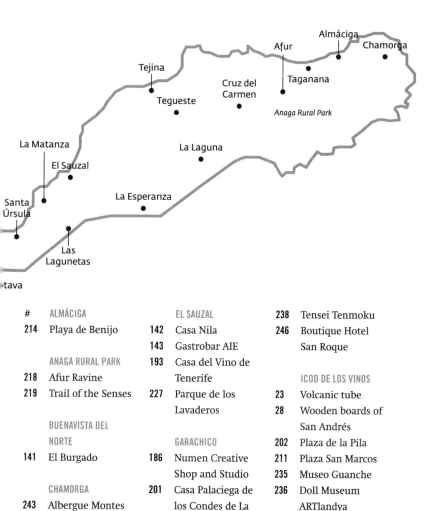

Almáciga
Chamorga
Afur
Tejina
Cruz del Carmen
Taganana
Tegueste
Anaga Rural Park
La Matanza
La Laguna
El Sauzal
La Esperanza
Santa Úrsula
Las Lagunetas
tava

PLAYA DE BENIJO

EAT

DRINK

SHOP

BUILDINGS

DISCOVER

CULTURE

C

SLEEP

Lip-smacking **FOOD**
served **WITH A VIEW**

---

139 **EL CALDERITO DE LA ABUELA**

Carretera Provincial 130 Santa Úrsula
+34 922 301 918
tripicotea.com

To pay tribute to their grandmother, who had a modest eating house, two grandsons recuperated granny's traditional recipes and named their cosy place 'Grandma's little cooking pot'. By adding a modern twist, the stews, the rabbit, the fish have all become surprising. Spectacular vistas of Puerto de la Cruz do the rest.

140 **LAS AGUAS**

C/ La Destila 20 San Juan de la Rambla
+34 922 360 428
restaurante lasaguas.wordpress. com

This family business was founded in 1983, in a very beautiful neighbourhood popularly known as Las Aguas. It's nicknamed 'Los Arroces', so it's easy to guess what their speciality is: rice and fish. Other great choices are Andalusian fries and seafood casseroles. A faultless venue with good food, friendly staff and fantastic views.

141 **EL BURGADO**

Playa de las Arenas Buenavista del Norte
+34 922 127 831
restaurante elburgado.com

The setting alone makes it worth the trip. Used in several commercial spots and movie scenes, El Burgado completely merges into its environment. Sitting on top of lava stones right by the edge of the water, tables occasionally get sprayed by the waves. Enjoy their excellent fresh fish and seafood. For dessert and coffee take a stroll to the slick adjacent golf course designed by Severiano Ballesteros.

142 CASA NILA

C/ La Iglesia 2
El Sauzal
+34 922 099 864

It's not easy to find the perfect meat restaurant on the island, but meat-lovers will rejoice as they get to choose their cuts, the size and which part of the world they want their beef to come from. Not exactly the cheapest place, but the food along with its fine setting and the minimalistic traditional interior make this a place to remember.

142 CASA NILA

CANARIAN CUISINE
with a twist

---

143 GASTROBAR AIE

Av. Inmaculada
Concepción 58-A
El Sauzal
+34 922 560 582

Omar Bedia is a young chef who promotes a fresh and modern cuisine, with a strong influence of Canarian culinary traditions. His restaurant is a little jewel serving elaborate small dishes and tapas. A favourite dish is the 'Pelibuey Lamb Gyozas'. Pelibuey is an autochthonous hornless breed of sheep with straight hair instead of curly wool.

144 EL GUAYDIL

C/ Dean Palahi 26
La Laguna
+34 922 266 843
restauranteguaydil.com

Guaydil's interpretation of real Canarian cuisine is very creative. They have high-quality food using only organic products. Paying special attention to a gluten-free menu, this is a great choice for gluten intolerants. Although located in the historic centre of town, the interior has a modern alternative feel to it hereby exhibiting some unique local artwork.

145 EL HUERTO

C/ Tabares de
Cala 12
La Laguna
+34 922 252 337

Another modern and stylish *tasca* with lots of personality, set in a beautifully restored two-storey town house in the old part of La Laguna. It's a place where meat-eaters and vegetarians happily join hands. Prices are very reasonable, with the possibility of ordering only half portions in order to try out more items on their exquisite menu.

146 ATUVERA

C/ Juan de Tejera 2
Puerto de la Cruz
+34 922 380 081
atuverarestaurante.es

A place to feed all of the senses. Set in a lovely converted Canarian mansion with delightful gardens to sit outdoors, this haven of relaxation is made for romance. A lot of care is put into presentation and taste, with a good choice of wines at affordable prices. Comfort food at its best. Go for the slow cooked melt-in-the-mouth lamb or pork.

147 EL TALLER DE SEVE DÍAZ

C/ San Felipe 32
Puerto de la Cruz
+34 822 257 538

The façade of this humble Canarian house is in sharp contrast with the contemporary chic you'll encounter once you step inside. Although they don't offer an extensive menu, exceptional creative well-presented cuisine is what to expect at this modern high-quality restaurant. Their six-course inventive tasting menu is worth a try. Book well in advance.

GUACHINCHES
– eat like the locals

---

148 CASA LITO
C/ Tijarafe 35
Santa Úrsula
+34 630 590 007

Originally *guachinches* or 'food houses' were created by the wine farmers' need to sell their surplus production. Allowed to serve up to three different dishes to accompany their wines, the farmers opened small rooms or garages on their premises, where they could cater to their customers. Nowadays, the northern countryside is strewn with more or less adapted *guachinches* offering local wine and the most homely Canarian broths. Casa Lito is a good place for an introduction; their speciality is barbecue meat.

149 EL PARRALITO
C/ San Cristóbal 66
La Matanza
+34 655 526 240

A very authentic *guachinche* located in the lower part of the owner's house, where a few tables have been roughly put down. In the corner some space is reserved for a small bar and kitchen. The blackboard tells you what's on the menu. There's only a limited choice, no grilled meats, but this is the real deal.

150 LA MORRA
C/ Las Rosas 34
La Esperanza
+34 676 307 390

One of our favourite no rush, no fuss, come-with-your-friends *guachinches*, serving Canarian potages, goat's meat, grilled meats, fantastic croquettes, desalted cod, and all kinds of truly authentic products of the land. Don't miss the famous 'La Morra salad', with *gofio* (flour made from roasted cereals), honey, dried fruits and goat's cheese.

151 CASA PEDRO EL CRUSANTERO

**C/ Magallanes 38,
Urb. Casablanca
Santa Úrsula,
Cuesta de la Villa
+34 922 300 082**

For many years clients from all over the island have visited Casa Pedro to enjoy a traditional Canarian *puchero* accompanied by an *escaldón de gofio* (see chapter 'Things to know'). *Puchero* is a very tasty complete menu consisting of chickpeas, big vegetable and maize cub chunks, cooked slowly with different types of meat, potatoes and sweet potatoes.

IBERIAN HAM, VINO & TAPAS

152 TASCA EL TONIQUE

C/ Heráclio
Sánchez 23
La Laguna
+34 922 261 529
tascaeltonique.es

Walking down the steps upon entering this old-fashioned traditional *tasca* founded in 1989, you'll be welcomed by the sweet smell of the Iberian hams hanging behind the bar. All along the walls of the cosy wooden interior you'll find bottles of the country's best bodegas: a fine selection of cava, red and white wines, giving you that authentic Spanish *tasca* experience.

153 TASCA EL OLIVO

C/ Iriarte 1
Puerto de la Cruz
+34 922 380 117
tascaelolivo.eatbu.
com

For a more updated *tasca* version, El Olivo in Puerto de la Cruz is a must-try. Considered as one of the best in town, there is indoor as well as outdoor seating to taste the wines and the marvellous tapas they are most famous for. The Canarian black pudding with almonds, the *padrón* peppers and the octopus with mashed potatoes are all worth a try.

154 MESÓN LA HIJUELA

C/ Herradores 104
La Laguna
+34 922 254 109
bodegalahijuela.com

It is impossible to walk past this beloved *Mesón* without getting a whiff of the luring smells of Serrano ham filling the air. This venue, which has an extensive wine list and serves tapas, belongs to the winery La Hijuela. The harvest of their own vineyards is a wine called 'Híboro', gold medal finalist at the 2016 AWC-Vienna Wine Challenge.

155 EL JAMÓN DE MOISÉS

Av. Obispo Benítez de Lugo 52
La Orotava
+34 673 527 993

Simplicity and sticking to the well-known, that is the key to success at this little restaurant serving pure *jamón ibérico de bellota* (Iberian acorn ham), grilled meats, Spanish *tortillas*, *paellas*, *pucheros* and other popular dishes prepared in an honest way and based on the family recipes. The wine list is original and well-adapted to the menu.

OCEAN FRESH

156 LA COFRADÍA DE PESCADORES

C/ Las Lonjas 5
Puerto de la Cruz
+34 922 383 409
*lacofradiade
pescadores.es*

This traditional restaurant, referring to the fishermen's guild and situated right by the dock, is one of the most popular in Puerto de la Cruz. Famous for serving the purest fish and seafood, you can either sit inside or enjoy the colourful harbour vistas on the large exterior terrace. Notice the nearby cute bronze statue of the shouting female fishmonger.

157 RESTAURANTE PLAYA CASA ÁFRICA

Roque de las
Bodegas 3
Taganana
+34 922 590 100

At some 100 kilometres from the South, this eatery is worth the trip. The food, though simple, tasty and fresh, is second to driving through the awesome *Anaga* biosphere reserve and finding this stunning coastal area in the upper north-eastern corner of the island. Casa África is totally in tune with this very authentic part of Tenerife. A must-go.

158 LA PIMIENTA

C/ Tosta de San
Antonio 70
La Matanza
+34 922 578 167
*restaurante
lapimienta.com*

This venue has over 30 years of experience and is extremely popular with residents. Upon entering you pick your fish and decide whether you want it grilled, boiled or fried. *Vieja, Bocinegro, Medregal, Cabrilla, Salmonete* are but a few names of the typical choice at hand. Famous is also the accompanying avocado salad. Take special notice of their opening times.

156 **LA COFRADÍA DE PESCADORES**

VEGGIE-VEGAN
lunch and brunch

159 SOMOS LO QUE COMEMOS
**Túnel Aguere,
C/ el Juego 14
La Laguna
+34 673 758 293**

'We Are What We Eat' is the name of this small family-run vegan restaurant situated in a passage near the old centre of La Laguna. For an economic price you can order a daily changing menu: starter, main and dessert. The food is fresh and resembles authentic Canarian food, but the menu is meatless.

160 TAPASTÉ
**Plaza San
Cristóbal 37
La Laguna
+34 822 015 528
*tapaste.es***

This specialised vegetarian restaurant only opens for lunch; it's small and very popular, so make sure to reserve your table. Their hallmark is completely homemade healthy food omitting all kinds of colourants or preservatives. Want to be a vegetarian but don't know where to begin? They offer personalised one-hour courses on nutrition.

161 EL LIMÓN
**C/ Esquivel 4
Puerto de la Cruz
+34 922 381 619**

El Limón with its quaint marine-style décor has been around for over 20 years, and is one of the pioneers in the vegetarian field. It's known for its salads and veggie burgers and its large choice of juices, smoothies and shakes. They also serve inexpensive daily lunch menus and a selection of (mostly) vegan cakes. Perfect for a quick lunch.

164 **MAKIKA & CO**

Charming places to satisfy a
S W E E T   T O O T H

---

162 CAFE VISTA PARAISO

C/ Vista Paraiso 21,
La Puntilla
Santa Úrsula
+34 922 300 612

Drinking coffee is part of the lifestyle in Tenerife. A fabulous place to fully enjoy your coffee, together with a big slice of cake, goes under the well-deserved name, Vista Paraiso. The cafe is a veranda with a viewing balcony high above the sea, run by Austrian Germans since 1969. Try their hot cinnamon apple tart with vanilla ice cream and fresh cream.

163 CASA EGÓN – TERRAZA VICTORIA

C/ del León 5
La Orotava
+34 922 330 087

Step back in time and admire this old-fashioned cake shop that has been serving traditional cakes and pastries since 1916. They have the best orange *millefeuille* in the world. Head for their Victoria Terrace with your coffee and pastry, to overlook the layered and well-trimmed Victoria Gardens with its intriguing white-marble mausoleum.

164 MAKIKA & CO

C/ San Juan 15
La Laguna
+34 922 891 830
makika.es

Put your feet up at this cosy and lush inner courtyard garden, covered in winter with a suspended fabric roof. They serve all types of coffees and teas together with a marvellous selection of fine homemade cakes and pastries. The atmosphere is young and innovative at this highly recommended little gem in the centre of the city.

Sunset-cocktail
TERRACES

---

165 ALBERTO'S BAR
Vía de Malpais 5
Puerto de la Cruz
+34 922 386 061

Alberto's is the perfect place for a cool cocktail while watching the sun go down. Tourists are seldom seen at this hidden off-the-beaten-track cafe with its sunny terrace high up on the hill and its uninterrupted views of the northwest coast. It lies at the end of a cul-de-sac in Taoro Park, a wonderfully lush elevated zone, excellent for nature lovers. Check out the romantic Risco Bello Gardens whilst in the area.

166 TERRAZA SUNSET 290
Urbanización
Vista Paraíso
La Orotava
+34 645 515 579

The hippest and most exotic terrace on the island for relaxed sunset-gazing, perched on a rugged mountainside overlooking the sea and surrounded by nature. You either walk to get there or use the shuttle offered by the venue. Once there, it feels like landing on another continent, no doubt due to the mystical oriental decor. There's a diverse food and cocktail menu, with frozen mojito at the top of the list. So as to feel even more comfortable, rent one of their Balinese beds.

NIGHTTIME PUBS
with special events

---

167 PUB AÑEPA
SALA DE ARTE

C/ Rosales 13
La Orotava
+34 922 331 277

An Orotava nighttime classic within the historic city centre. Evening drinks and art come together at this emblematic Canarian house that has been offering culture to the town for over 30 years. You'll find cold beer and cocktails, great music, an occasional live concert, a nice patio and original art exhibitions in a place that's open when the rest of the town is asleep.

168 BLANCO BAR

C/ Blanco 12
Puerto de la Cruz
+34 620 955 197
blancobar.com

A lively cocktail bar with terrific music in a variety of styles continuing into the wee hours. There's a good Canarian atmosphere, with a discotheque in the lower area, while the upstairs terraced zone is quieter, allowing for a drink, a talk and a smoke. Popular events such as live music concerts, comedy plays and magic shows take place regularly.

169 EL RINCÓN
DE TINTÍN

Plaza de la
Concepción 7
La Laguna

El Rincón de Tintín is located in a small alley in the historic centre of La Laguna. There are two bars: one is dedicated to cocktails only and the other one is for beer. The picturesque environment with its stone walls and a small Canarian courtyard is a popular nighttime meeting place, where various types of musical acts frequently come about.

170 ANDERSON GAY PUB AND SHOW BAR

Av. Betancourt y Molina 24
Puerto de la Cruz
+34 922 966 734
andersongaybar.com

The audience at this long established evening bar, which offers parties and events, is mostly gay, but everyone is welcome. The most popular acts are the cabaret performers with drag queen shows, go-go dancers and male strippers, every Friday and Saturday night. A friendly atmosphere with a mixed/gay crowd.

171 CAFÉ QUILOMBO

Plaza del Quinto Centenario
C/ Cantos Canarios 9
La Orotava
+34 669 863 624

Not only a pub where you can quietly sit and talk, with well-selected music playing in the background, but also a mystical concert-hall at the weekends. It's a groovy place to come to with music-loving friends. Some of the best performances on the island have taken place here. A *quilombo* was a space where a fugitive slave was free.

COSY TAVERNS
to enjoy with friends

---

172 BODEGÓN TOCUYO
C/ Juan de Vera 16
La Laguna
+34 922 250 045

Wine barrels and bottles everywhere, along with the hanging rows of cured ham and the writings on the wall left by happy drinkers, this is one of Tenerife's temples where friends cosily meet. A very charming and authentic bar to try out the best *almogrote* (typical cheese paté from La Gomera) with a plate of excellent Serrano ham and a glass of wine.

173 TASCA LATOPA
C/ Heraclio
Sánchez 27, Edf.
Galaxia
La Laguna
+34 822 662 825

A hidden gem! This is a small, atmospheric and alternative tavern where insiders gather in the evening. A friendly place to enjoy a chilled drink and an exquisite tapa. Depending on the day of the week, the boys at the bar prepare food from different countries; Tuesdays and Wednesdays are sushi nights.

174 HANNEN ALT BAR
Plaza del Charco 1
Puerto de la Cruz
+34 922 371 383

A well-known beer garden on the corner of Plaza del Charco that has been around for donkey's years, but never ceases to please. Ideal for German-beer-lovers. Sit outside to enjoy some people watching, although inside it's probably cosier. If you're hungry, try their succulent steak or their *Mett* (German bread with minced raw pork, served on a wooden board).

DAYTIME BARS
at exceptional locations

---

175 BAR TENO ALTO (LA VENTA)
AT: **Parque Rural de Teno**
C/ Los Bailaderos
38489 Teno Alto
+34 922 693 060

At the end of a long scenic drive you'll find this tiny hamlet where time hasn't moved on. People come here for two reasons: fresh local goat's cheese and wine. The bar can barely be called a bar, but the generous and warm-hearted Cipriana will make you want to stay longer than you had planned. No wonder most inhabitants become centenarians at this beautiful hidden spot, unvisited even by many *Tinerfeños*.

176 EL RISCO
C/ La Hoya 9
San José de los Llanos
+34 922 136 867

It will take some searching to find this creative spot, hidden within the dense greenery on the hillside above San José de los Llanos. In an area famous for hiking, the bohemian flavour is dominantly present at this cabin-like unconventional little bar, run by two women serving good homely food. Check Facebook for their live music events.

177 BAR BLANKY CASA FIDEL
C/ Lomo del Medio
Masca
+34 922 863 457
blankymasca.com

The gorge of Masca is hiked by many, no doubt due to its unequalled beauty. At the tip of the ridge, at the spot where the trail starts, you'll find the ever-smiling Blanky, ready to serve you the world's best *barraquito* or a fresh squeezed juice. If she's not too busy ask her to bring out the *timple* (a local string instrument) and sing an old Canarian song.

VINTAGE, ANTIQUES *and* DESIGN *at La Laguna*

178 ADC VINTAGE&DESIGN

C/ Ascanio y
Nieves 1
La Laguna
+34 686 725 913
adcvintage.com

If you love stylish designer items from around the mid-20th century, visit this small shop dealing in furniture, lighting and decoration from days gone by. At their salesroom, in the historic city centre, you can lay your hands on original articles mostly imported from Denmark, Italy and France.

179 DICKY MORGAN

C/ San Agustin 75
La Laguna
+34 922 267 064

Vintage has become a lifestyle for those who wish to dress in an exclusive and free-spirit way, standing out from the main stream. At Dicky Morgan you'll bump into vintage secondhand as well as new clothing, with timeless items to fill your wardrobe. Epoch decoration objects and furniture give the shop its authentic flair.

180 PLASTIC PEOPLE

C/ Viana 25
La Laguna
+34 922 265 639

After visiting a London pub called 'Plastic People', the owner decided to use this name for her urban style shop targeting a male audience. It's a space where English and Nordic brands, made by small but exclusive designers, can be found together with accessories, decoration and vintage articles at reasonable prices.

181 ANDERSON& MALAQUITA

C/ Alfredo Torres
Edwards 4
La Laguna
+34 922 190 597

A beautifully arranged small antiques and vintage shop, to search for that exquisite little object you always wanted to have. Nice porcelain and glassware, fine jewellery, sun-mirrors, an original collection of porcelain swallows, small furniture and many other delicate items make this an enjoyable place to drop by.

182 LA RESTAURADORA DE LA LAGUNA

C/ Bencomo 20
La Laguna
+34 922 254 472
*larestauradorade
lalaguna.com*

The motto of this inventive store consists of the 3 R's: 'Restore, Reuse and Recycle'. A local craftswoman started this project: she recuperated tables, chairs and desks from the garbage and gave them a new life. Their unique showroom, stocking many items from the previous century, is also a workshop teaching the necessary techniques to make-over. Only opened on Fridays and Saturdays.

179 **DICKY MORGAN**

Buying ARTS AND CRAFTS

183 ARTENERIFE
(various locations)
C/ Tomás Zerolo 34
La Orotava
+34 922 334 013
artenerife.com

The central objective of Artenerife is to promote locally produced handicrafts, with a sharp eye on quality. New and existing crafts are encouraged at this island-wide chain store trading in creative jewellery, ceramics, soaps, embroidery, paintings, glass and any other handmade-in-Canarias art that fits their high-standard framework.

184 LA RANILLA ESPACIO ARTESANO
C/ Mequinez 59
Puerto de la Cruz
+34 629 553 069
laranilla.org

La Ranilla, the old fishermen's quarter of Puerto de la Cruz, and now known for its vibrant street art (see map at intersection Calle Mequinez and Calle Perez Zamora indicating where to find 17 murals), is a super area to go shopping for unique gifts. The cottage painted a flashy turquoise is where you'll discover all kinds of innovative local arts and crafts. Also check out their exhibitions and events.

185 DON'T PANIC
C/ Tabares de Cala
15, local 7
La Laguna
+34 922 265 284
dontpanic.es

Walking into this store feels like entering a mini art exhibition with original work of local designers and illustrators. At this imaginative clothes and gift shop there is only one condition: everything must be high quality and handmade. At their workshop they will also personalise or transform any object you want them to take care off.

186 **NUMEN CREATIVE SHOP AND STUDIO**

C/ Francisco Martínez de Fuentes 2-A Garachico
+34 922 830 708
numencreativeshop.com

Positioned in the historic centre of Garachico, Numen showcases contemporary Canarian artists and designers. At this creative space they have a nice choice of designer pieces, limited editions and selected special items including contemporary photography, paintings, jewellery, sculptures, hats/hat gear and bags.

185 DON'T PANIC

LEATHER SHOES *and* BAGS
made in Spain

187 ABRAHAM ZAMBRANA TENERIFE
Urbanización el
Drago 28
La Orotava
+34 636 650 748

Award-winning designer from Jerez called Abraham Zambrana, moved to Tenerife, where he created his own brand. He makes luxury handmade leather men's shoes, unisex bags, briefcases and suitcases fit for a king. His items take 3 to 4 weeks to finish and have been seen on many a catwalk. Pop into his showroom to have a look for yourself.

188 PISAVERDE
C/ Juan de Vera 7
La Laguna
+34 922 314 128
pisaverde.org

In 2013 this couple from La Laguna won the National Craftsmanship Award for their original and colourful handmade shoes and bags. Specialising in women's shoes, their items are characterised by overlaying pieces of leather with different patterns. Exclusive designs in anything from boots to high-heeled sandals and sports shoes.

189 LURUEÑA
Plaza del Charco 2
Puerto de la Cruz
+34 922 383 983
luruena.es

This historic company started in 1952 and has two well-known stores on the island: in Santa Cruz and in Puerto de la Cruz. A traditional high-quality shoe shop for both men and women, delivering stylish and elegant leather shoes with matching bags. They specialise in party shoes and casual flat pumps for daily wear.

Shopping for
LOCAL DELICATESSEN

190 DEPATANEGRA IBÉRICOS

Av. de Canarias 7
La Orotava
+34 630 857 248

The most succulent (and expensive!) Iberian ham, called *Pata Negra*, comes from pigs exclusively fed on acorns. The stock at this quality shop includes a wide range of Spanish hams with denomination of origin, sausages and cold meats, fine wines along with excellent cheeses and other gourmet products.

191 MERCADO MUNICIPAL

Plaza del Cristo
La Laguna
+34 922 253 903

The best way to stock up on local specialities is to check out this popular covered market with its rich choice and its overwhelming smell of fresh produce. Go from stall to stall to pick out the local produce like honey, wines, cheeses, dried fruits, dried fish, jams, *mojo* sauces, sweets and spices. Heaven for foodies.

192 LA CATEDRAL

C/ San Juan 1
La Laguna
+34 922 259 126

This old-fashioned bakery and cake shop, open since 1914, is one of the city's classics. It gets its name from La Laguna Cathedral, situated opposite the store. Here you can buy the famous *laguneros*, *rosquetes* and *truchas*, typical pastries loved by the locals. *Truchas* with a sweet potato filling (*batata*) are very tasty.

193 CASA DEL VINO DE TENERIFE

C/ San Simón 49
El Sauzal
+34 922 572 535
casadelvinotenerife.com

A place not only to buy, but also to try. This old hacienda has been carefully restored and houses an appealing wine and honey museum. At a small price wines and cheeses can be sampled before buying what you like at the giftshop. There are also interesting gardens that introduce you to a vineyard and the local flora. Stay for coffee and cake or have lunch in or outdoors. A great spot to spend a few hours. Don't miss the ceiling of the hermitage.

194 MIRADOR DE GARACHICO

TOURIST TAT

at nice locations

194 MIRADOR DE GARACHICO

C/ San Juan del
Reparo 54
San Juan del
Reparo
+34 922 830 294
*miradorde
garachico.com*

Tenerife is true tat-heaven, and to be honest, who hasn't succumbed to the odd fridge magnet, snowball or 'I love Tenerife' T-shirt, exclusively made in China? If it's a holiday souvenir you're after, here you'll have plenty of choice, but don't forget to look over the edge towards the sea for a spectacular bird-eye view of Garachico!

195 RESTAURANTE LA FUENTE

C/ Lomo del Medio
Masca
+34 922 863 466

It's the biggest bar in Masca, boasting a fantastic terrace overlooking one of the most spectacular gorges in Tenerife. At this three-in-one venue you can eat, drink or buy colourful cheapness and everything will be settled at the same till by Pepe, the owner. Without pushing it, he will also cut you one of the island's tastiest slices of almond cake.

196 CASA DE LOS BALCONES

C/ San Francisco 3
La Orotava
+34 922 330 629
casa-balcones.com

'The House of the Balconies' is the most touristy place in La Orotava, no doubt due to the stunning woodwork adorning this historic magnificent mansion. Of course, a lot of people attract a lot of commercial business, but this is one of the only surviving places where to buy the genuine – not made in China – Canarian lacework and needlework.

CONTEMPORARY ARCHITECTURE *up North*

197 AIRPORT TERMINAL LOS RODEOS

La Laguna
+34 902 404 704
aena-aeropuertos.es

The N-3 group of architects is at the base of this functional building with its high-end architectural quality. Far from being a box with geometric volumes, the terminal with its rounded shapes has been incorporated into the silhouette of the mountains that surround it. Its defined and arcuate forms have given this bright structure an overall personality.

198 SANTÍSIMO REDENTOR CHURCH

C/ Volcán
Estromboli 3
La Laguna

This vanguard parish church was designed by Fernando Menis, who also has several other projects to his name in the South. The mystical aspect of the building is conceived by its austerity and the angle of the light. A large ramp, which is part of the structure, resolves the different levels of the plot. The design is part of the MoMA (Museum of Modern Art) permanent collection in New York City.

199 FACULTY OF FINE ARTS

AT: Campus de Guajara
C/ Radio Aficionados
La Laguna
+34 922 319 741

Designed by GPY Arquitectos, the Faculty of Fine Arts is a nice example of New Architecture. It stands out by its spectacular curved shapes in the form of multiple loops. This large construction measuring over 32.000 square metres was modelled for artistic studies and exhibitions and is made of reinforced concrete and cast glass. The building won the International Architecture Award 2015.

Famous HISTORIC CASAS

200 CASA LERCARO

C/ del Colegio 5-7
La Orotava
+34 922 330 629
casalercaro.com

There's plenty to entertain the eye at this traditional architectural jewel, built in the 17th century and catalogued as a Cultural Interest Site (BIC). The regal mansion belonged to a Genovese family of traders who moved to Tenerife after the conquest. The house, courtyard and gardens are open to visitors. There is a cafeteria/restaurant and a nice decoration shop.

201 CASA PALACIEGA DE LOS CONDES DE LA GOMERA

C/ Francisco
Montesdeoca y
García 3
Garachico

The Palace House, which belonged to the Counts of La Gomera, was built in the 16th and 17th century. It is also called the Stone House because of the stone-clad façade, intended to impress the common people. Situated along the main *plaza*, the house had to be restored after the volcanic eruption of 1706, which largely destroyed the town of Garachico.

202 PLAZA DE LA PILA

Plaza de la
Constitución
C/ Arcipreste
Ossuna 1
Icod de los Vinos

Plaza de la Pila, also a BIC site, gets its name from the fountain holding a *ñame* plant and standing in the centre of the square. The construction of this *plaza* started in 1631. Look out for the beautiful balconies and the carved woodwork of the surrounding houses. The biggest house is the 19th-century Lorenzo Cáceres Palace House, now a cultural centre with a library and exhibition rooms.

203 CASA SALAZAR

C/ San Agustin 28
La Laguna

The erection of this Palace House, which became the episcopal palace in the 19th century, was started in 1664 by the Salazar family. Sadly the original house (now rebuilt) with all its artistic treasures burned down in 2006, leaving only the façade, which is considered by many to be the finest example of a baroque façade within the Canarian civil architecture.

Inspiring things to do in
LA LAGUNA

204 FREE GUIDED CITY WALKS

AT: **Tourist Information Office**
C/ Obispo Rey Redondo 5
La Laguna
+34 922 631 194
turismodelalaguna. com

Made a UNESCO World Heritage Site in 1999, La Laguna is the first example of an unfortified town with a grid pattern, forerunner of the later settlements in the New World. With its many classified buildings there is a lot to explore in this living historic centre. Call the given phone number, or pop into the office to find out about the one-hour guided tours in various languages.

205 PARQUE PEDRO GONZALEZ (EX-PARQUE LA VEGA)

C/ Concepción Salazar 5
La Laguna

The park was named after Pedro Gonzalez (1927-2016), renowned painter and ex-mayor of La Laguna. With its 22.500 square metres, it has a rich variety of trees, a lake with over 80 different species of aquatic plants and water lilies, sports elements among which a rockdrome, a skatepark, a BMX circuit and ping-pong tables. Together with its kiddies area and cafetaria, it is a good place for a great family outing.

206 MUSEUM OF HISTORY AND ANTHROPOLOGY OF TENERIFE

C/ Agustin 22
La Laguna
+34 922 825 949
museosdetenerife.org

This museum has a lot to offer; the building alone, dating from the 16th century and built by the Italian merchant family Lercaro, is already worth the visit. Other highlights include Guanche pottery and traditional crafts. The house is supposedly haunted by the Lercaro daughter who lived here a few centuries ago and killed herself on the day of her arranged wedding.

LA LAGUNA

SUNNY PLAZAS
to relax and watch the world go by

207 PLAZA DE LA LIBERTAD
Garachico

An elevated square in the middle of the town, flanked by historic buildings and two churches. An art nouveau bandstand/cafeteria, a bronze statue of Simón Bolívar, exotic flowers and trimmed little lawns make out the dreamlike setting where the older generation is often seen resting, drinking coffee and playing cards under the lush centenarian ficus trees.

208 PLAZA DEL CHARCO
Puerto de la Cruz

Plaza del Charco is the heart of the old town. It is a huge animated *plaza* next to the old port with lots of palm trees, a children's playground and a big cafeteria. Its name comes from the *charco* (puddle of seawater) that used to form in the middle of it. Plenty of excellent restaurants are found in the Ranilla district behind the square. Superb ice cream at Freddino's.

209 PLAZA DE LA CONSTITUCIÓN
La Orotava

Presenting an original bandstand and cafeteria, this plaza has some striking *Cassia Spectabilis* trees offering gorgeous autumn flowers blooming bright yellow. Go for some sightseeing around the square and visit the palace-like Liceo Taoro, showing off its splendid gardens, and the 17th-century San Agustín Church with its adjoining ex-convent. When standing in front of the church's main altar, look up at the ceiling to see the surprising high-relief woodcarving of Nuestra Señora de Gracia.

210 PLAZA DE LA LUZ
Los Silos

The village square and its 20th-century octagonal, double floored art nouveau kiosk are a must-stop for all visitors to Los Silos. These elements are linked to the town's fiestas and popular traditions. In September expect folklore festivals, cultural acts, fanfares, expositions, concerts and outdoor cinema to take place here.

211 PLAZA SAN MARCOS
Icod de Los Vinos

Plaza San Marcos, right next to the island's oldest dragon tree (*Dracaena Draco*), is a favourite with nature and history lovers. The 16th-century San Marcos Church stands in the middle of the square and houses invaluable treasures among which the world's largest silver filigree cross and a maize paste Christ-figure made by Mexican Indians in the 16th century. The surrounding gardens have amazing plants and trees from various continents.

207 PLAZA DE LA LIBERTAD

Stunning **BLACK BEACHES**

212 PLAYA DE EL BOLLULLO
Puerto de la Cruz

Different and exotic, generally smaller and rockier than golden beaches, black beaches tend to get very hot under the feet. At this isolated *playa* you'll find a 160-metre principal beach and an adjoining 60-metre cove. To get there, take the exit 'Puerto de la Cruz – El Rincon'. Along the way there are various restaurants, but the *chiringuito* on the beach is definitely more fun.

213 PLAYA EL SOCORRO
**Ctra. del Socorro
Los Realejos
*tenerifeplayas.com/
webcams-tenerife***

Here we encounter one of the 12 beaches adapted for wheelchair users and offering a wide array of facilities. This 230-metre-long beach is also popular with surfers and bodyboarders and sometimes on summer evenings films will be shown. To find out more about actual bathing conditions on the island, use the given link, which uses more than 20 webcams to keep track of real-time weather at different locations.

214 PLAYA DE BENIJO
Almáciga

Situated in the northwestern corner of the island and far away from any of the tourist centres, there is this wildly spectacular 300-metre savage beach. A place in a million with aesthetic surroundings that are hard to beat. All good things come with a price though and caution is advised when the sea is rough. Access is from the road, via a 15-minute stepped trail, next to El Mirador restaurant. Visit at low tide to enjoy a large surface of black sand.

214 **PLAYA DE BENIJO**

A dip in a **NATURAL POOL**

215 **CHARCO DE JÓVER**
Camino Playa de
Jóver 8
Tejina

The rugged northern coastline has few beaches but lots of nooks and crannies. Seawater enters those irregular shapes to create natural crystal clear pools. The family-friendly pool of Jóver is popular with residents and has been adapted to make it suitable for people with reduced mobility. Other family-oriented pools are in Bajamar and Punta del Hidalgo.

216 **CHARCO DEL VIENTO**
La Guancha
(Santa Catalina)

As ancient lava flows reached the ocean and hardened, a small natural bay was formed between the lava tongues. This isolated natural pool, with its constant roll of fresh seawater, is situated in an agricultural area with lots of banana plantations. There is an access road leading off the TF-5 at km 48 that will take you to a parking place. Don't forget your snorkeling gear. Equally marvellous is the nearby Charco de la Laja in San Juan de la Rambla.

217 **EL CALETÓN**
Av. Tomé Cano
Garachico

The quaint town of Garachico should definitely be on your list of must-visits. Not only its beauty and history will enthral you, but also its twisting lava pools; a result of the 1706 volcanic eruption, when lava flows creeping towards the ocean largely destroyed the town. Take a dip and then enjoy a seafood paella on the terrace of restaurant La Almena, overlooking El Caletón.

216 **CHARCO DEL VIENTO**

Get-back-to-nature **HIKES**

218 **AFUR RAVINE**

START AT:

**Visitors' Centre
Cruz del Carmen
Carretera Las
Mercedes, km 6
La Laguna
+34 922 633 576**

Setting off in Afur, a mountain hamlet in the Anaga Rural Park, this fantastic hike leads down the Afur gorge to the unexploited Tamadite beach. The ravine is home to a wealth of endemic fauna and flora and plenty of impressive geological structures. Plan an early start as you will need the time to walk back up again or to border the coast reaching Taganana. Before you take off, get some extra info at the stated Visitors' Centre.

219 **TRAIL OF THE SENSES**

START AT:

**Visitors' Centre
Cruz del Carmen
Carretera Las
Mercedes, km 6
La Laguna
+34 922 633 576**

If you are looking for a suited family-hike, follow the educational Trail of the Senses through the fairy-tale laurel forest. It starts at the Visitors' Centre Cruz del Carmen and has three different sections according to length and difficulty. The easiest part is adapted to prams and wheelchairs. The most difficult passage is suited for older children and takes you to the stunning viewpoint of Llano de los Loros.

220 **TENO RURAL PARK**

START AT:
Visitors' Centre
Los Pedregales
El Palmar
+34 922 447 974
rutasteneriferural.
com

Very few natural areas have such a well-organised network of signposted and well looked-after trails. A good place to find out about the routes that match your needs is at the Visitors' Centre Los Pedregales situated in the El Palmar valley. They also provide guided hikes, to be booked in advance. For a good selection of self-guided rural trails on the island check the website.

220 TENO RURAL PARK

Divert **OFF THE BEATEN TRACK**

221 **LA TIERRA DEL TRIGO**
lossilos.es

Not very well-known and somewhat hidden lies the small village of La Tierra del Trigo (Land of the Wheat). A hair-raising way to get there is from the coastal town Los Silos, via the Camino Real las Arenas road; one of the steepest and most winding roads on the island. The other access road is via El Tanque. Situated at 500 metres height, this is an unspoilt agricultural area with vineyards, potatoes and fruit trees. Well worth the effort if you are looking for the authentic Tenerife.

222 **LOS SILOS**
lossilos.es

With its elegant *plaza*, Los Silos is an excellent place for a coffee break before heading down to its coastal area. Although a bit out of the way, this quiet spot is good fun, providing a series of natural rock pools (if the tide is not too high), as well as municipal pools, bars and restaurants. *Balaenoptera Borealis* is the type of whale whose skeleton was used to make an impressive six-metre-long sculpture located by the seafront.

223 TEGUESTE

tegueste.es

Tegueste is a small agricultural municipality with a surprising architectural and natural patrimony. Its historical centre was declared an Asset of Cultural Interest in 1986. The highlight though is the quality of its wines. More than 30 varieties of grapes are cultivated here, to produce excellent wines in the numerous wineries of the region, with the denomination of origin 'Tacoronte Acentejo'. If you enjoy wine-tasting, this is obviously a place to take into account. Farmers' market on Saturday and Sunday mornings.

LUSH GARDENS
to get lost in

224 JARDÍN BOTÁNICO

C/ Retama 2
Puerto de la Cruz
+34 922 922 978
icea.es

Created in 1788, this popular garden has an important collection of tropical and subtropical plants with huge ornamental as well as economical value. Most outstanding are the many trees that are either antique, unique, exotic, or enormous. The absolute prize piece is the incredible Lord Howe fig tree (*Ficus macrophylla f. columnaris*) in the centre of the garden.

224 JARDÍN BOTÁNICO

225 JARDÍN DE ORQUÍDEAS DE SITIO LITRE

Camino Sitio Litre s/n
Puerto de la Cruz
+34 922 382 417
jardindeorquideas.com

This historic British garden with its lovely collection of orchids, was first created by the Little family (hence its slightly transformed name) who moved into the adjoining mansion in 1774. It has seen many famous and legendary faces smell its flowers: Alexander Von Humboldt, Sir Richard Burton, Marianne North, Agatha Christie...

226 HIJUELA

C/ Tomás Pérez 6
La Orotava
+34 922 330 050

La Hijuela is related to the Botanical Garden in Puerto de la Cruz. It's a 3390-square-metre public garden situated behind the Orotava town hall, incorporating a lot of Canarian flora. At the entrance you'll find a beautiful specimen of *Dracaena Draco* (dragon tree). Amongst the exotic flora there is a magnificent *Ginkgo Biloba*, an ancient species dating back 270 million years.

227 PARQUE DE LOS LAVADEROS

C/ Los Lavaderos s/n
El Sauzal
+34 922 570 000
elsauzal.es
>turismo>parques

Situated at 200 metres above sea level and near the San Pedro Apóstol Church, lies this 8000-square-metre recreative area designed around a natural source that was used for washing laundry in olden days. Its beautiful gardens, waterfalls, paths and lookouts towards the north of the island make this a relaxing place to discover.

Places to look at
CONTEMPORARY ART

228 **ESPACIO DE ARTE CASA DE PIEDRA**
Glorieta de
San Francisco
Garachico
+34 922 830 000
areagarachico.com

This attractive contemporary art space is located inside the former 17th-century home of the Counts of La Gomera, characterised by its beauty and its stone façade. Temporary pictorial as well as sculptural and audio-visual exhibitions of Canarian artists take place here all year round. This art space is connected to TEA (see chapter 'Santa Cruz').

229 **MUSEO DE ARTE CONTEMPORÁNEO EDUARDO WESTERDAHL (MACEW)**
C/ Las Lonjas,
Casa de la Aduana,
1st floor
Puerto de la Cruz
+34 922 381 490
iehcan.com/inicio/macew

Located in the remarkable Customs House, built in 1620, the permanent exhibition comprises around 60 works divided over four rooms. Work of outstanding Canarian masters such as Óscar Domínguez, César Manrique, Manolo Millares, Juan Ismael, Pedro González a.o. shares this space with artwork of other national and international artists. Eduardo Westerdahl himself was a Canarian surrealist painter, as well as a writer and an art critic.

230 GALERÍA BRONZO

C/ Nuñez de la
Peña 19
La Laguna
+34 922 267 176
esculturasbronzo.
com

The Galería Bronzo is one of the references for sculptural art in Tenerife. Various sculptors using metal and other materials expose here and their creations are sold amongst other artistic work. Bronzo also strongly promotes contemporary jewellery made by Canarian designers, hereby inviting several artists to create a special piece of jewellery for their yearly exhibition of Designer Jewels.

231 GALERÍA DE ARTE ARTIZAR

C/ San Agustín 63
La Laguna
+34 922 265 858
artizar.es

This gallery opened in 1989, focussing on promotion of Canarian contemporary art. As time moved on they have expanded their vision to include Latin-American artwork, especially from Cuba (e.g. Manuel Mendive), as well as to incorporate national and European artists from various countries, e.g. Dave McKean, Laura Gherardi, Hans Lemmen.

230 GALERÍA BRONZO

Important
YEARLY FESTIVALS

232 MUECA STREET ART FESTIVAL
Puerto de la Cruz
festivalmueca.com

Every year around the second weekend of May, this joyous international arts festival is held in Puerto de la Cruz. During four intensely animated days the public is able to enjoy and participate in many original high-level street shows. During the festival new masterpieces of street art are created. The party programme is extended well beyond midnight in the many venues, bars and restaurants.

233 FESTIVAL BOREAL
Los Silos
festivalboreal.org

This alternative international eco-event takes place in September in the historic centre of Los Silos. The aim of the festival is to spread the importance of caring for the environment. Recycling workshops, the release of turtles, an eco-tourism fair, craft markets, food fairs, exhibitions and music concerts are but a few of the typical activities anyone can freely engage in during this four-day fiesta.

234 TENERIFE WALKING FESTIVAL
Puerto de la Cruz
tenerifewalking festival.com

For anyone passionate about walking and the outdoors, 20 different hikes falling into 3 categories (coastal, volcanic and forestal) have been mapped out to show people the beauty of the island. Puerto de la Cruz, in its role as base-camp, additionally offers a wide variety of supporting activities. Since 2015, this notable hiking event is held in May.

Museums suited for **K I D S**

235 MUSEO GUANCHE

AT: **CC La Magalona**
C/ Pepe Floro 5-7
Icod de los Vinos
+34 922 191 004
museoguanche.com

A place where the actual world of the Guanches, the original inhabitants of Tenerife, becomes real through recreations of their daily activities in ten different settings, hereby exhibiting life-size dolls. Without being a great museum or a remarkable exhibition, Museo Guanche sheds a light on the pre-Hispanic historical and cultural past of the island and its people. Visually interesting for kids.

235 **MUSEO GUANCHE**

236 DOLL MUSEUM ARTLANDYA

Camino el Moleiro 21
Icod de los Vinos
+34 922 812 615
artlandya.com

This is a museum for contemporary doll art, entertaining for children as well as for grown-ups, with fascinating handmade dolls and teddies by various international artists. The museum is set in a quiet, picturesque and renovated Canarian country house. The Austrian owners spared no effort to make this a magical little wonderland.

237 MUSEO DE LA CIENCIA Y EL COSMOS

Av. Los Menceyes 70
La Laguna
+34 922 315 265
museosdetenerife.org

'Learn while you play' is the message at the Museum of Science and the Cosmos. Inaugurated by the Russian astronaut Sergei Krikalev in 1993, it resembles an interactive amusement park: more than 70 experiments, such as turning your face into a skull, lifting a car with one finger and getting lost in a mirror maze, help us understand the laws of our universe. Highly recommended.

MONUMENTAL
SCULPTURES *worth visiting*

238 TENSEI TENMOKU
BY KAN YASUDA
**Anda Tome Cano
Garachico**

'Door without Door' by Japanese artist Kan Yasuda is a minimalist sculpture consisting of two separate frames made out of white Carrara marble. Its geometrical setting against the intense blue Canarian sky and ocean makes this an intrigueing work, used by many visitors as background for an original holiday snapshot.

238 TENSEI TENMOKU

239 LA GIGANTA

Jardín Social
La Quinta
Av. Los Pesqueros
13
Santa Úrsula

This curious fairy-tale sculpture was created when the Santa Úrsula town council commissioned the creation of a vertical garden for the cultural festival SU Guiño in 2013. The result was a 4-metre-tall giantess, appearing in a sitting position, fused into a heap of rocks. Some of her body parts are made of concrete while others are covered in plants.

240 MENCEY BENTOR

BY CARMEN LEÓN
RODRÍGUEZ
Mirador de El
Lance TF-342
C/ Icod el Alto 6
Los Realejos

In 1496 the Guanches, led by Bentor, lost the last battle against the Spanish conquerors. Distraught Bentor, stripped of all his clothes and amulets, decided to commit suicide by jumping off the cliff. With this bronze statue of Bentor, capturing the moment before he jumps, the Canarian artist created a very moving image.

CHEAP SLEEPS
in fantastic hiking areas

241 HOTEL RURAL FINCA LA HACIENDA

C/ Nuestra Señora
de Lourdes 2
La Tierra del Trigo
+34 636 136 513
fincalahacienda.com

The exceptional location of this family-run hotel, in a farm surrounded by fruit trees, will allow you to discover a very privileged and authentic rural environment. The *finca* comprises a set of nine various-sized basic apartments with kitchenette. Hearty homemade food can also be ordered from the more than friendly owner Baudilio, who is the perfect example of Canarian hospitality.

242 ALBERGUE BOLÍCO

AT. Parque Rural
de Teno
Camino los
Charcos s/n
38480 Las Portelas
+34 922 127 938
alberguebolico.com

As well as catering for singles and couples, this state-owned hostel is also frequented by families and all kinds of organised groups. Its beautiful location and its vicinity to some of the best hikes on the island (e.g. Masca ravine, Teno Rural Park), together with its excellent facilities and services, make this a popular place with athletes, students and nature-lovers in general.

243 ALBERGUE MONTES DE ANAGA

Carretera El
Bailadero
Chamorga
+34 922 823 225
alberguestenerife.net

At this hostel, also state-owned, the setting and the views are simply priceless. There are nine small rooms, fitted with either 2, 4 or 6 bunk beds. The common areas where breakfast, lunch and dinner are served, are spacious and functional. Various outdoor activities are offered in order to fully enjoy what is considered as one of the Canary Islands' most beautiful natural environments.

243 ALBERGUE MONTES DE ANAGA

CHIC and NOBLE *hideouts*

244 HOTEL EMBLEMÁTICO SAN AUGUSTÍN

C/ San Agustín 18
Icod de los Vinos
+34 922 813 194
hotelsanagustin.es

Canarian hotels only receive the emblematic stamp if the building is historical, further having cultural or artistic elements that revalue it. Here six of the eight rooms are configured around a typical island-style inner patio in a beautifully restored ancestral home, built in 1736. The hotel is located in the centre of the town Icod de los Vinos, a fairly unexploited place with a rich history and lots of secrets to discover.

245 LA LAGUNA GRAN HOTEL

C/ Nava y Grimón 18
San Cristóbal de
La Laguna
+34 922 108 080
lalagunagranhotel.
com

This historic townhouse was built in 1776. Keeping its Canarian character and charm, it has recently undergone a de luxe renovation and is now part of a new, modern hotel in the centre of the city. The 22-metre rooftop pool provides great panoramic views overlooking La Laguna and its surroundings, whilst its acclaimed restaurant, called Nub (*nubrestaurante.com*), was recently awarded a Michelin star.

246 BOUTIQUE HOTEL SAN ROQUE

Esteban
de Ponte 32
Garachico
+34 922 133 435
hotelsanroque.com

The former 17th-century sophisticated and stately mansion that belonged to the prominent Ponte family, restored with an innovative spirit between 1992 and 1996, is listed as a historic building. The result is a stunning combination of modern art and traditional architecture with unique art work by artists such as Charles Rennie Mackintosh, Mies van der Rohe, Le Corbusier, Susi Gómez and Carmen Calvo among others. An obligatory stop if you enjoy beauty and elegance at its best.

246 BOUTIQUE HOTEL SAN ROQUE

C A S U A L *and* C O S Y *places to sleep*

247 HOTEL RURAL OROTAVA

Carrera del
Escultor Estévez 17
La Orotava
+34 922 322 793
hotelruralorotava.es

Famous since 1994 for its patio-restaurant Sabor Canario serving typical traditional food. In 2003 this old mansion (dating from 1595 and one of the oldest mansions in La Orotava) was rehabilitated as a hotel, presenting seven nicely decorated rooms on the upper floor, showcasing authentic wooden floors and ceilings. Tranquil and full of tradition this hotel is well located to discover the beauty of one of Tenerife's most historic towns.

248 CASA RURAL LA ASOMADA DEL GATO

C/ Anchieta 45
La Laguna
+34 922 263 937

This peaceful and homely decorated guest house is located in a protected building and only minutes away from the pedestrian historic zone of La Laguna. The quaint inner courtyard is cosy and filled with exotic plants, flowers and trees. Its friendly owners and staff are very helpful and intend to make you feel welcome during your stay.

249 HOSTAL B&B LA LAGUNA

C/ Juan de Vera 21
La Laguna
+34 822 173 608
bblalaguna.com

A brightly coloured, fresh and cosy guesthouse where guests choose to sleep in either a double room or in a shared room with 4 to 6 bunkbeds. A unique and fun little place, popular with the younger generation. The very homely environment provides a shared kitchen and lounge and an outdoor leafy patio with lemon and orange trees, the fruit of which can be picked by guests in February.

3

MOUNT TEIDE

Throughout history many great scientists have been enthralled by the natural wonders the Canary Islands harbour. Even Charles Darwin, who had ardently planned to visit Tenerife but unfortunately through circumstances never made it, was fully aware of this oceanic island's unique biosphere.

Nowadays the Canarian fauna and flora have acquired significant fame and universal recognition. Most striking are the lizards and the large numbers of dolphins and whales living in the surrounding waters. Besides the animals, the archipelago is also home to a variety of endemic plants. Many of these endemisms, such as the Canarian pine and palm trees, can be found in all or several of the islands, whereas others are exclusive to one single island. In this aspect Tenerife's unique king of spring is the spectacular Red Tajinaste flower (*Echium Wildpretii*), the symbol of Teide National Park.

The National Park automatically leads us to volcanoes. Although centrally located Mount Teide (3718 m) is one of the biggest and most impressive volcanoes in the world (and should by no means be skipped), it is certainly not the only one on the island. Over millions of years and in various episodes, the island itself has been created by innumerable volcanoes and eruptions, resulting in breathtaking cliffs, mountains and ravines. Adventurous hikes along the countless winding roads and paths, will allow you to fully explore this beautiful territory and will leave many a true nature lover in absolute awe.

MOUNT TEIDE

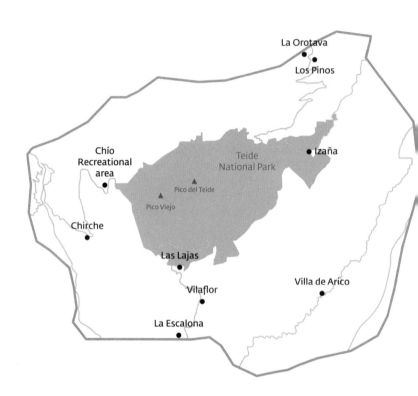

VIEW FROM THE SOUTHWEST

EAT

DISCOVER

SLEEP

RANDOM

Eating amongst VOLCANOES

---

250 RESTAURANTE MARMITIA PARADOR LAS CAÑADAS DEL TEIDE

Las Cañadas
del Teide
Teide National
Park
+34 922 386 415
parador.es

Come here if you fancy some fine dining after your hike. Situated inside the state-owned Parador hotel, the outstanding beauty of this location is hard to beat. The restaurant enjoys wonderful views of the third largest volcano in the world. It's not especially cheap, but you'll get a complete menu of the finest local cuisine. In winter, savour your after-dinner drinks in front of the open fireplace.

251 RESTAURANTES EL PORTILLO AND LA BAMBY

Ctra. General
Las Cañadas
Teide National
Park
+34 922 356 006
portillobamby.es

Two different venues owned by the same people and open 365 days a year. Both restaurants have surprisingly stuck to homemade, fair-priced local food which is offered to the more than 4 million guests visiting the National Park each year. Try their Spanish *tortilla*, always hot and freshly made, or simply drop by for a coffee and an ice cream.
To the back of El Portillo you'll find an easy walking trail suited for children, which nametags the endemic flora.

252 RECREATIONAL AREAS: LAS LAJAS AND CHÍO

LAS LAJAS AREA: **Vilaflor TF-21, km 58,2**

CHÍO AREA: **Guía de Isora TF-38**

Especially on Sundays or on holidays, many local families take out the picnic basket and head for Mt Teide to enjoy nature at its best. Las Lajas and Chío, located just outside the National Park, are picnic spots set in the scented Canarian pine forest. They provide wooden tables and benches, barbecues, running water, toilets and a playground for kids. If the islanders' lively joie-de-vivre should not appeal to you, choose to go mid-week. Great spots for bird-watching.

250 RESTAURANTE MARMITIA PARADOR LAS CAÑADAS DEL TEIDE

Different **ACCESS ROADS**
driving up to Mt Teide

253 **FROM THE SOUTH VIA VILAFLOR ON THE TF-21**

There are four main access roads to the National Park. An average of 1 hour and 20 minutes is what it takes to get there. Driving up the winding south road has the following advantage: a visit to the picturesque Vilaflor, one of Spain's highest villages, surrounded by potato fields, almond trees, vineyards and wineries. Try their typical *tortas de almendras* (almond cookies) and stop by at 'El Pino Gordo': the thickest pine tree of the archipelago.

254 **FROM THE SOUTHWEST VIA CHÍO ON THE TF-38**
RESTAURANTE
MIRADOR DE CHIRCHE
C/ Era Rompida
Chirche
+34 922 850 525

This scenic, moderately winding road, is ideal for your descent. If weather conditions are favourable, you'll witness the impressive *mar de nubes,* a natural phenomenon where a sea of clouds creates an unbelievable sight. With some luck, you might even spot the three western Canary islands (La Gomera, La Palma and El Hierro). Along the way, stop at Chirche, a small hamlet where time seems to have stood still. Enjoy a great lunch with a stunning view at Restaurante Mirador de Chirche.

255 FROM LA LAGUNA VIA LA ESPERANZA ON THE TF-24

Making your way up from the North, you'll drive through La Esperanza wood, a temple of the majestic Canarian pine tree. This is a perfect spot for nature lovers, offering a myriad of walking and biking trails. A few child-friendly barbecue and picnic spots, such as Las Raices or Las Calderetas, provide fun areas for families. This is a road with many amazing viewpoints and striking vistas of the imposing volcano and the Izaña Observatory.

256 FROM THE NORTH VIA LA OROTAVA ON THE TF-21

BODEGÓN DE MATÍAS
Ctra. General
Parque Nacional
del Teide
Los Pinos –
La Orotava
+34 686 485 028
bodegonmatias.es

Due to the great panoramic views of the ocean with its famous sea of clouds and the huge Orotava Valley, this road is more suited for driving downwards. On your way you'll see a little gift of nature called 'La Margarita de Piedra', a curious geological basalt formation resembling a flower. At the end of the road stop to have lunch or dinner at the quaint restaurant Bodegón de Matías, serving hearty Canarian food and a delicious *mousse de gofio*.

A *visit to the* **SUMMIT**

257 **TEIDE CABLE CAR**

Ctra. General
Las Cañadas
Teide National
Park
+34 922 010 440
volcanoteide.com

With its 3718 metres above sea level Mt Teide is the third largest volcanic structure in the world. Any visit to the island is incomplete without exploring it. You can either choose to stay at the base or to ascend its cone. The most comfortable way to go up is by cable car, taking you to viewpoint La Rambleta at 3555 metres. Get an online fast-track ticket as queues tend to get quite horrendous.

257 TEIDE CABLE CAR

258 TELESFORO BRAVO TRAIL

*reservasparques
nacionales.es*

If you wish to hike the remainder (about ½ hour) to the peak and experience the fumaroles and sulphur smells of this live volcano, you'll need to follow the Telesforo Bravo trail. Important: you must present a free of charge access permit, issued by the National Park's administration and best applied for many weeks or months in advance. Requests can be made online.

259 ALTAVISTA MOUNTAIN REFUGE

AT: **El Teide
Teide National
Park**
+34 922 010 440
volcanoteide.com

Those who prefer the full Monty and wish to walk from the base to the crater (about 6 hours), are in for a very unique experience. Your best option is to set off early afternoon from the Montaña Blanca trail, sleepover at the Refugio Altavista (cabin hut at 3260 metres, charging 21 euro pp.) and climb further up early morning, in time for an unforgettable sunrise. No need for an access permit if you ascend before 9 am. Timely reservation at the refuge is essential.

Original ways to **EXPLORE**

260 **BY HELICOPTER**

C/ Charfa 2 - Las
Torres
Adeje
+34 922 711 487
*helidream
helicopters.com*

Maybe not the cheapest way to scout the island, but certainly one of the most thrilling. Taking a look at the volcanos, cliffs and ravines in bird's-eye view is popularly exploited by filmmakers and photographers. On a more romantic note though, it has been used as a unique occasion to 'pop the question'.

261 **BY FERRARI**

Av. El Palm-Mar 2
Palm-Mar
+34 603 110 316
*luxurycarhire
tenerife.com*

Sports cars are at their best on sunlit, twisting and winding mountain roads and there are plenty of those around on the island. If driving a Ferrari, Lamborghini, Porsche or Bentley makes your heart tick, then this is the perfect time and place to tick this item off your bucket list.

262 **BY HARLEY DAVIDSON**

Av. Rafael Puig
Lluvina 22
Playa de las
Américas
+34 664 116 299
*canaryislandsrides.
com*

Tenerife is the ultimate biker's paradise. Enjoyable all year round, it offers a meandering road-network through an amazing variety of landscapes. Either rent a bike and go solo or choose a guided tour. If you can't ride, hop on the back and let a guide do the work. Insurance, helmets, gloves and jackets are supplied.

Adventurous **HIKES**

263 **37 DIFFERENT TRAILS**

National Park Office
+34 922 922 371
gobiernodecanarias.org>Teide>Rutas

The National Park has an extensive maze of 37 approved and signposted trails, classified into different categories according to the level of difficulty and length. Choose between self-guided or free-of-charge guided hikes. Either call the National Park Office or send an email (*teide.maot@gobiernodecanarias.org*) to book a guided route in advance or attend the information centres available in the Park for additional information on your chosen walk.

264 **ALTO DE GUAJARA**

A 2-km linear hike with starting point at Degollada de Guajara (trail 5), including a high level of difficulty and an incline of 325 metres. The Alto de Guajara with its 2715 metres is the highest crest of the caldera's wall, which almost entirely encircles Mt Teide. Find the ruins of astronomer Jean Mascart's hut at the summit. This is where he studied Halley's Comet in 1910.

265 **ROQUES DE GARCÍA**

This 3,5-km circular walk, rising 175 metres and classed medium difficulty, surrounds the famous Roques de García. On your way you'll see the less frequent *pahoehoe* flows, forming smooth and domed pillow-lavas or twisting ropey lavas. Also enjoy the diverse endemic flora on this trail. Springtime, when the park is filled with all kinds of spectacular coloured blooms, is undoubtedly the best time to visit. Tenerife's pride is a unique flower called *Echium Wildpretii* or Red Tajinaste, reaching up to 2 metres.

265 ROQUES DE GARCIA

STARGAZING

266 NATIONAL PARK LAS CAÑADAS DEL TEIDE

Have you ever seen the Milky Way? Along with Chile and Hawaii, the National Park is one of the world's best stargazing spots. Unpolluted, practically cloud free skies, with the Sahara to one side and the broad Atlantic to the other, provide the perfect conditions. From Mt Teide it's possible to see 83 of the 88 constellations annually presented by the starry skies. Dress warmly and take a blanket to beat the cold.

267 TEIDE OBSERVATORY

Izaña
+34 922 329 110
iac.es

An arrangement of white domes silhouetted against the intense blue horizon is where the astrophysical and meteorological observations take place. It is one of the world's most important observatories, counting on international collaboration. Check their site for open-door visits and free use of the Mons Telescope, available for astronomy students and amateurs. Guided visits are organised by *volcanoteide.com*.

268 STAREXCURSIONS

starexcursions.com

José Antonio Paris, an accredited and very knowledgeable Starlight guide, will join you on an interesting small-scale private tour to Mt Teide, explaining and pointing out the stars in our galaxy. His infectious enthusiasm will make sure that in one evening you will learn more about astronomy than in all your years at school.

269 VOLCANO TEIDE EXPERIENCE

+34 922 010 444
volcanoteide.com

Tenerife's most exclusive stargazing tour is called 'Sunset and Stars on Teide'. After ascending by cable car to 3555 metres, you'll see Spain's highest sunset followed by a cocktail dinner designed by a renowned Michelin-star chef. A Starlight guide will then help you discover planets, galaxies and clusters by the use of professional telescopes. Other astronomic tours are also available.

267 **TEIDE OBSERVATORY**

Cool VISITORS' CENTRES

270 VISITORS' CENTRE TELESFORO BRAVO

C/ Doctor Sixto
Perera Gonzalez 25
La Orotava
+34 922 922 371

Telesforo Bravo was an outstanding Canarian geologist, considered by many as the father of volcanology on the Canary Islands. This centre, best visited prior to driving up to Mt Teide, is situated in La Orotava, at 25 kilometres from the Park. It is undoubtedly a must for those wanting to get to know Teide National Park in detail. Free of charge and closed on Mondays.

271 VISITORS' CENTRE EL PORTILLO

Parque Nacional
Las Cañadas del
Teide
TF-21, km 32,1
+34 922 922 371
gobiernodecanarias.
org>Teide>Centros
de Visitantes

An information centre containing a small, free of charge didactic museum, recreating the interior of a volcanic tube. A good place to learn about geological, botanical, zoological and archaeological aspects of the Park. Visit the annexed botanical garden and find out about the endemic flora. Free guided hiking tours are on offer; reservations are essential. Toilets available.

272 ETHNOGRAPHIC MUSEUM JUAN ÉVORA

Parque Nacional Las Cañadas del Teide
TF-21 and TF-38 Boca Tauce junction
+34 922 922 371
gobiernodecanarias.org>Teide>Centros de Visitantes

Juan Évora was the last official inhabitant of Las Cañadas (end of the 1980s), maintaining the traditional way of life. The little house in which he lived has been transformed into a small ethnographic museum exhibiting the customary lifestyle of shepherds in this area. Free entrance; toilets available.

ADRENALIN SPORTS
for the adventurous

273 PARAGLIDING HAPPY FLY TENERIFE
Camino la
Hondura 17
La Escalona
+34 639 384 124
*happyflytenerife.
com*

Glide in an exciting and safe way on a breathtaking tandem flight. Requested to sit upfront, you'll be guided by experienced staff in order to fully enjoy this adventure in a relaxed manner. Their top flights take off at Teide National Park and land in Puerto de la Cruz. Should you become addicted, courses are available.

274 ROCK CLIMBING
Tenerife Climbing
House
C/ La Asomadita 8
Villa de Arico
+34 689 886 809
*tenerifeclimbing
house.com*
ocho-escalada.com

Authorised climbing in the Park is possible, with popular spots at La Cañada del Capricho and La Catedral. Other favourite climbing areas on the island are Arico, Anaga and Risco de Guaria. Stay at the Climbing House or camp on their grounds to find out more or to team up with fellow climbers. In partnership with El Ocho climbing school they offer courses and excursions with certified guides for all levels.

275 CANYONING AND ABSEILING

Canyon Tenerife
C/ Tenerife 10
El Médano
+34 600 792 052
canyontenerife.com

This is an animated way to see the most hidden corners of the island. Benjamin, a passionate and skilled guide, will let you experience action-packed abseils, world-class views and aquatic as well as dry canyoning adventures. No need to worry about gear and transport, it all comes included.

276 SKYDIVING

+34 626 331 588
aventuraencanarias.com

Jumping out of an airplane may not be exactly everyone's idea of having fun, but skydivers recommend we should all give it a try at least once in a lifetime. In a place where the weather is unbeatable and the views are awesome, either get on a tandem jump or subscribe to a course and plunge on your own.

274 **ROCK CLIMBING**

Comfy or rough
MOUNTAIN SLEEPS

277 PARADOR DE LAS CAÑADAS DEL TEIDE

Las Cañadas
del Teide
Teide National Park
+34 922 386 415
parador.es

Very few hotels in the world are able to beat the location of this luxury lodge-style, state-owned hotel. As soon as daytime visitors and tour groups leave the National Park, you'll have the surreal landscape and starry skies all to yourself. A telescope for guests' use is available and on Friday evenings at 10.30 pm there is a guided stargazing session for hotel residents.

278 PRIVATELY-OWNED MOUNTAIN HOUSES

Casa Tajinastes del Teide
Casa Siete Cañadas
La Casa del Teide

In the sixties, contrary to modern policies, a few private houses were built in the area of El Portillo, within the boundaries of the National Park. Some of the owners have made their houses available for holiday lets. Only through major booking sites will you be able to get a hold of them. Perfectly located if you want to be close to nature; electricity and running water can be scarce.

279 EL REFUGIO ALTAVISTA

El Teide
Teide National Park
+34 922 010 440
volcanoteide.com

To stay the night at this 3270-metre-high refuge, you will be completely pulled out of your comfort zone. No showers, no frills, except a bunk bed with clean sheets and a warm duvet. No food either, except from the snack dispenser and a kitchen to heat the food you have brought. But all this is a small price to see the most spectacular of sunrises at the top of Mt Teide. The grandest experience on the island.

SURPRISING FACTS

280 3718 METRES

At 3718 metres above sea level Mt Teide is Spain's highest peak. Measured from the bottom of the ocean, it is the planet's third largest volcano in height and volume, following the Hawaiian giants Mauna Loa and Mauna Kea. On Tenerife the last volcanic eruption took place in 1909, from a volcano called Chinyero.

281 1000 PESETAS NOTES

The old Spanish bank notes had a beautiful picture of Mt Teide and Roques de García imprinted on them. The most famous and original rock is called Roque Cinchado or 'The stone tree'. It's a 27-metre-high layered volcanic rock that has eroded to a monumental shape. A two-hour circular trail will take you around the formation.

282 THE ICE CAVE

Measuring 11 by 7 metres and situated near the Altavista Mountain Refuge, this cave holds ice all year round. Now it is only visited by the curious few, but in olden days *los neveros* or ice dealers extracted ice and transported it on donkeys and mules to the villages, where it was sold. The first written references date back to 1792.

283 AXIS MUNDI

The Guanches, the aboriginals living on Tenerife before the Spanish conquest, mummified their dead and believed in the immortality of the soul. For them *Echeide* (Mt Teide) was a Holy Mountain, an *Axis Mundi* or the connection between Heaven and Earth. *Echeide* was also Hell, the place where *Guayota,* the god of evil, lived.

Extra info for

VOLCANO LOVERS

---

284 THE CALDERA

There are many reasons why volcanologists from all over the world adore this Park. Apart from the enormous stratovolcano (built up by many layers), there's also the caldera, one of the largest on earth. This is a huge 16-by-9-kilometer elliptical wall-like structure with a maximum depth of 600 metres, practically surrounding the volcano.

285 ROQUES DE GARCÍA

Roques de García is situated opposite the Parador Hotel. Going back in history these strange eroded rock formations are leftovers of the first grand volcanic structure occupying this space. Unable to support its own weight, the original edifice collapsed and slipped towards the sea, thus forming the huge caldera.

286 OBSIDIAN BLOCK-LAVA FLOWS

There are different types of lava flows in the Park. The most spectacular ones are near Montana Rajada: broken up into enormous blocks, topped with a thick layer of shiny black volcanic glass called obsidian. Obsidian was used by the aboriginals to make cutting tools called *tabonas*.

287 LAS MINAS DE SAN JOSÉ

The pumice banks at Minas de San José are the result of very violent explosive eruptions. As pumice has many applications in construction, cosmetics, horticulture, etc., they were exploited up until the 1980s. Nowadays the banks, resembling landscapes from Star Wars planets, are a fantastic area to stroll or to make exquisite photographs.

288 THE NOSTRILS OF MT TEIDE

Pico Viejo (3135 m), right next to Pico del Teide (3718 m), last erupted in 1798. This eruption left an eerie, black barren lava field of five square kilometres. Those lavas can be traced back to two large crater holes on the southwestern side of Pico Viejo, called the nostrils of Mt Teide.

288 PICO VIEJO

4
THE SOUTH

After the Spanish conquest of Tenerife in 1496, the newly acquired territory was taken from the aboriginals (Guanches) and divided amongst the newcomers. The vast and barren southern parts of the island, where water was scarce and crops were difficult to grow, were considered as land that nobody wanted. But lo and behold, in the 1960s with the introduction of tourism, the whole southern area, with its minimal infrastructure and its cachet of being a poor and distant region, started to experience an enormous metamorphosis.

In the years to follow a whole series of projects and investments were developed in order to take advantage of the extensive coastline marked by beaches of remarkable quality. Nowadays the south of Tenerife is one of Spain's most important tourist zones as well as being the motor of the island's economy.

According to taste and budget, there are many options to choose from: laidback El Médano, especially popular with wind and kite surfers; Costa del Silencio, which has the most crystal clear waters; Los Cristianos, which still maintains a fishing village feel to it; Playa de las Américas, famous for its many shops, bars, restaurants and buzzing nightlife; upmarket Costa Adeje with its sophisticated lustre and its ample variety of luxury facilities; and of course the quiet Los Gigantes, named after the impressive cliffs dominating the resort. And for those looking at different alternatives, there are the many private *casas rurales* dotted all over the island.

EL MEDANO KITE SURF

EAT

DRINK

SHOP

BUILDINGS

DISCOVER

CULTURE

SLEEP

ACTIVITIES

Tasty **BREAD** and **CAKES**

289 **100% PAN Y PASTELERÍA**

C/ La Graciosa 4
Playa San Juan
+34 922 138 247

Located in the undisturbed coastal town of Playa San Juan, this small bakery has been rewarded as one of the three best bakeries in Spain. The extremely creative owner, a third-generation baker, truly surprises with his finger-licking avant-garde desserts. Either take away or eat on their small terrace, where you can have breakfast or a light lunch.

290 **AROMA PASTEL-ART CAFÉ**

C/ Francisco
Alfonso Güitima 1,
Edf. Duque de la
Torre
Arona
+34 922 726 331
pasteleriaaroma.es

The Aroma bakery, situated at 600 metres high in the historical town of Arona, will surely satisfy your sweet tooth. Not only do they serve a wide selection of delicious homemade pastries and cakes, but also a range of freshly-made baguettes. The real reason to pay them a visit, though, are their scrumptious *millefeuille* pastries, filled with custard and whipped cream.

291 **DINKELBÄCKER**

Av. Tenbel 30
Las Chafiras
+34 922 735 626
dinkel.es

In other words, the Spelt Baker. This is the place to look for whole grain, first-rate bread in all shapes and sizes, using different types of cereals. Their choice of mouth-watering sweets contains some typical German specialities such as the classical apple strudel, the seedy poppy cake or their healthy muesli bar filled with nuts and honey.

Exclusive DINING
WITH A STAR

292 EL RINCÓN DE JUAN CARLOS

Pasaje Jacaranda 2
Los Gigantes
+34 922 868 040
*elrinconde
juancarlos.com*

The two Padrón brothers, running this gem with their mother and spouses, have a well-deserved Michelin star to their name. Each dish is delicately put together and offers a feast to the eyes and the palate. With excellent value for money, they have created their very own style, respecting the gastronomical traditions of the island. Highly recommended.

293 ABAMA KABUKI

Ctra. General del
Sur 47, km 9
Guía de Isora
+34 922 126 000
*restaurantekabuki.
com*

The Kabuki Group, boasting a Michelin star, is known as a meeting point between Mediterranean and Japanese cuisines. At this vanguard restaurant, appropriately located at Tenerife's Ritz Carlton, the sushis and sashimis show off the purest of flavours and are then washed down with applaudable champagnes, wines or sakes. Remember to bring your wallet.

294 ABAMA MB

Ctra. General del
Sur 47, km 9
Guía de Isora
+34 922 126 000
*martinberasategui.
com*

A must-try for the foodie who's looking for the big budget blow-out experience. Also located at the Ritz, the MB restaurant is led by the famous Basque Chef Martín Berasategui and has earned itself two stars. Go for their Great Tasting Menu to give your taste buds a treat. You may need a while to select your drinks, as the wine and champagne list is endless.

Fresh **FROM THE SEA**

295 **AGUA Y SAL**

C/ Callao Hondo 22
San Miguel de
Tajao
+34 922 171 176
grupopiccolo.com

Tajao is a little hidden secret: a small undisturbed fishing village on the east coast, priding itself with a few fabulous fish restaurants. Upon arrival, choose your freshly caught fish and seafood from the large display at the entrance, add a chilled bottle of fine white, and experience the real Canarian savoir-vivre. Best to book in advance.

295 AGUA Y SAL

296 RESTAURANTE BAHÍA LOS ABRIGOS

C/ La Marina 40
Los Abrigos
+34 922 749 856
restaurantebahia.net

Have you ever eaten fresh fish made in a salt crust? Try this interesting dish at the Bahía, one of our favourite spots at the picturesque Los Abrigos bay. Other noteworthy specialities include seafood *paellas* and *fideuás* (similar to paella, but made with pasta). An ideal location for dinner, followed by a relaxing stroll on the promenade.

297 RESTAURANTE ABADES

C/ 16 de Mayo,
CC Abades
Abades
+34 922 090 065
restauranteabades26.
jimdo.com

In Tenerife you are spoilt when eating fresh from the sea – so many choices, but you should try this off-the-beaten-track little gem that does a unique grilled fish with a slightly smoked taste. This no-fuss restaurant with its huge windows offers unspoiled sea views while the locals, who have a nose for good eats, love it here.

Real Italian ICE CREAM

298 LA GOLOSA
(various locations)
Paseo Marítimo 11-B,
Edf. El Carmen
Los Cristianos
+34 922 791 855
grupoplaneta
goloso.com

This is the real thing. Well-known and loved by locals, this ice-cream shop will entice you with a large selection of 65 amazing flavours to choose from. Of course all naturally made, without colourants or additives. You can sit outside by the seafront promenade or you can take your cone for a walk.

299 GELATERIA EXOTICA
Litoral Fañabe
local 53
Costa Adeje
+34 922 719 639
www.gelateria
exotica.com

This has been a great family-run cafeteria since 1995: a place to admire the sea and the glorious sunsets, while savouring a delicious ice-cream sundae. The genuine Italian *gelato* is made solely with milk, sugar and fresh cream. Add to this a freshly brewed Italian coffee and the picture is complete.

300 VALENTINO
Rambla Dionisio
Gonzalez 17
Las Galletas
+34 922 734 094
valentinotenerife.com

Las Galletas wouldn't be the same without its popular Italian cafe selling craft ice cream and pizzas. Classical tastes like stracciatella and Málaga are presented besides more daring ones such as black chocolate with cherries or the bright blue variety called *chicle* (chewing gum). The nearby open-air gym will make sure you work off those extra calories.

Healthy **VEGGIE-VEGAN**

301 **SAMELO VEG**
Av. Marítima 4
Abades
+34 617 205 396

This strictly vegan, family-owned restaurant has a well-deserved reputation. Serving 100% homemade food, that's their key to success. Even the beer they sell is handcrafted, while the wines are organic. The taste of their natural food lures many non-vegetarians alike. Should your children come along, a kiddies corner is available.

302 **K-VEGAN**
AT: **CC Passarella Oasis**
Av. San Francisco 6
Los Cristianos
+34 922 794 885

Grab a bite at the vegan food stall inside the lively Pepa Food Hall. Their seaweed wrap is something to die for. The Pepa, with its communal vibe, provides shared long wooden tables, and sometimes even throws in some live music. A fabulous semi-outdoor venue for an informal eat, offering foreign and local cuisines to choose from.

303 **BUENAVIDA VEGAN**
AT: **CC Fañabe Plaza**
Av. de Bruselas 20, 1st floor
Costa Adeje
+34 922 715 752

A hit with all of our resident vegan friends, this is the place to savour fine gourmet vegan food which is purely organic and boasts excellent quality. Favourites are: the delicious burger and fries, the liquefied juices and the heavenly cakes. Their underground parking space is a huge asset in this busy area.

EAT *the* MEAT

---

304 CASA FITO

Ctra. General del
Sur 4
Chimiche
+34 922 777 279
casafito.com

Filiberto, a modest and self-taught chef, took over his father's humble *cantina* in the middle of nowhere and turned it into one of the best restaurants of the South. Proud to be an islander, he particularly enjoys making people happy... and you will be! Expect vanguard Canarian market cuisine with matured meats as their speciality. Check the opening times before heading out.

305 MESÓN CASTELLANO

Av. Antonio
Domínguez,
Residencial El
Camisón 38-39-40
Playa de las
Américas
+34 922 792 136
mesoncastellano.com

Always brimming with guests, this is an absolute must-try if you love meat. You'll find some glorious Castilian recipes on the menu, but go for the roast suckling pig or the unusual but delicious *Mollejas de Cordero*, consisting of lambs' thymus glands. The rice dishes are another must-eat and the wine selection is very complete.

306 RESTAURANTE LA ROMERÍA

**Ctra. General
Guaza a Las
Galletas TF-66, 218
Las Galletas
+34 922 691 272**

Although it might look like just another road restaurant, it's actually one of the finest in this area. Family-run, with a display case full of the best of meat, and a selection of top wines to be praised, owners Pili and Joachim know how to take excellent care of their clients. You will not be disappointed.

307 RESTAURANTE EL CORDERO

**Ctra. TF-652,
Guargacho–Las
Galletas
Las Chafiras
+34 922 734 171**

A huge sheep-shaped trimmed tree marks the entrance to El Cordero, which is located in a former greenhouse. Tasty grilled meat, typical Canarian decoration and an earthen floor make this venue extremely popular with locals. Although famous for its lamb's meat, other great dishes include steaks, ribs, Canarian blood sausages and *chorizos*.

304 **CASA FITO**

Good places for **L U N C H**

308 **LAS GANGARRAS**
Camino Machin 18
38627 Buzanada
+34 922 766 423
lasgangarras.com

Everything about Las Gangarras is really and truly Canarian. A series of small rustic houses, over 200 years old, were transformed into dining areas, exclusively serving authentic island cuisine. A relaxing spot to enjoy the surrounding gardens showcasing colourful bougainvillea's and tall palm trees. An ideal place to bring the kids along.

309 **LA PEPA FOOD MARKET**
AT: **CC Passarella Oasis**
Av. San Francisco 6
Los Cristianos
+34 922 794 885

Mentioned under veggie-vegan, Pepa Food Market is a place of plenty. Mexican, Asian, Venezuelan, hamburgers, sweets, juices or salads, it's all available and ready in a jiffy. Give your kids a shot at the on-site playground while enjoying your after-lunch coffee, or do some shopping at the Passarella shopping mall underneath.

310 **RESTAURANTE VARADERO VIEJO**
C/ Varadero 26
Las Galletas
+34 822 144 652
restaurante varaderoviejo.es

An unpretentious little fish restaurant specialising in fresh fish, which first opened in 2016, and quickly became beloved amongst the locals. Built almost on top of the beach, it enjoys a very privileged setting in Las Galletas, a small fishing village at a 15 minutes' drive from the main tourist areas. Try their appetizing *escaldón de pescado* as a starter.

Genuine CANARIAN TASTES

311 BAR RESTAURANTE ESPAÑA

C/ Grande 18
Adeje
+34 922 710 002

The main reason for people to drive up to Adeje for a meal, fully aware they'll be sitting on uncomfortable chairs plonked on a sloping pavement terrace, is *pollo frito con mojo*. Believe me, it's worth it. Never before will you have tried as good a fried chicken as this one, prepared with spicy, garlicky Canarian *mojo* sauce. There are more venues in the same street that all serve more or less the same dish.

312 EL DORNAJO

C/ El Hoyo,
La Escalona
Ifonche
+34 922 725 768

This is the perfect spot to indulge after you finish hiking in the unspoiled Ifonche area. Very popular with natives, this huge rustic place fills up at the weekends and is known to cook the best *conejo frito encebollado* (fried rabbit with onions) in the South. Leave some space for one of their finger-licking homemade desserts.

TASCAS, TAPAS and WINE

313 **TASCA EL HORNO**
C/ Virgen del Buen
Viaje 39
38616 Cruz de Tea
+34 922 771 486

An authentic Canarian *tasca*, serving excellent homely food and white wine of their own vintage. The atmosphere is welcoming, local and familiar. Sundays tend to be busy at this little secret place situated at the foot of the impressive forest crown and surrounded by vineyards, potato fields and almond trees.

314 **TASCA TIERRAS DEL SUR**
C/ de Pedro
González Gómez 20
Granadilla de
Abona
+34 922 771 482
*tascatierrasdelsur.
com*

Delicious food, fantastic wine, friendly staff and a quirky decor; what more could you wish for? Your best bet is to order a few of their outstanding tapas (let the waiter help you) and to enjoy a shared meal with lots of variety. A good selection of the best Spanish and Canary wines makes this experience complete.

315 **LA TASQUITA DE TOÑO**
C/ Camilo José
Cela 28
38632 Guargacho
+34 922 786 330

Quality is high on the list at this tiny local *tasca*, miles away from tourism. In fact, you would probably only end up here if a resident friend invited you. A little gem loved by insiders because of the good food, the friendly service and the cosy ambiance. Besides the tasty tapas, try the three-chocolate dessert.

BLUES, ROCK *and* REGGAE BARS

316 KING OF JUDAH
C/ Monaco 6
Los Cristianos
+34 666 017 531

Jay Rastafari! Entrancing reggae beats and comfy sofas with cosy African-print cushions will get you in the right mood to wallow in the reggae vibes. A homely place to indulge in conversations with bro's from around the globe, while smoking shishas or sipping exotic cocktails.

317 VEINTE 04 SURF CAFÉ
C/ Hermano Pedro 2
El Médano
+34 922 178 375
veinte04surfcafe.
business.site

El Médano square is the place to look for this lively casual-style surf bar, providing good homemade food and tapas. Live concerts, usually every Saturday and Sunday, offer a wide variety of different music styles including rock, jazz, funk, blues and reggae. A good setting for a night out with friends. Excellent cocktails.

318 MATINAL BEACH
Av. del Atlántico
(between Las
Galletas and
El Fraile)
Las Galletas

It's little more than a shack, hidden on a small beach between El Fraile and Las Galletas. On Fridays between 8 pm and midnight Latin-music lovers gather to dance under the stars. Check Facebook for their weekly live-music events with emphasis on local bands. Fill a cup with cigarette ends picked up from the beach and you'll get a free beer.

317 VEINTE 04 SURF CAFÉ

SUNNY TERRACES *with a view*

---

319 FLASHPOINT

**Paseo Nuestra
Señora Mercedes
de Roja 52
El Médano
+34 922 176 111**

A laidback cafe and terrace for all kinds of surfers and surf gazers to hang out. Right next to the famous kite beach, this place not only has animated views, but also offers a tasty and healthy menu with good breakfasts, salads, pastas and hamburgers. Another great choice is their hot apple strudel with ice cream.

320 EL NAÚTICO TERRACE

AT: **Hotel
El Naútico Suites
C/ San Miguel
Golf del Sur
+34 922 738 618**

Golf del Sur is known for its many British residents, hence our favourite place for the best tea and scones. The ample terrace with its unbeatable views of the Ocean is a great place to eat, drink and relax after a walk along this beautiful coastline. Famous for their tapas and burgers. Don't miss the Happy Hour between 5 and 7 pm.

321 EL MIRADOR ARCHIPENQUE

**Ctra. General
Puerto de Santiago
s/n
Los Gigantes
+34 922 862 951**

Overlooking the giant cliffs of Los Gigantes, this popular viewpoint offers a cafe with a hanging wooden terrace, a small gift shop and a telescope, magnifying the awesome view. Although most people only stop for a look, the sunny terrace is a relaxing spot to try out the wonderful coffee and homemade cakes.

EVENING COCKTAILS

a go-go

---

322 LA TERRAZZA DEL MARE
Av. Rafael Puig Lluvina
Costa Adeje
+34 922 796 498

A posh place with a seafront setting and good music. If you like romance, opt for a private *palapa* giving you some extra intimacy to enjoy a professionally prepared cocktail whilst the sun is setting and the sky is turning a deep orange. Their menu is a fusion of Asian and Italian cuisine, combined with select wines.

322 **LA TERRAZZA DEL MAR**

323 BAHÍA BEACH

Paseo Tucan 25
Palm-Mar
+34 822 141 225
bahiabeachtenerife.
com

Have a nice evening cocktail at this trendy chill-out beach club, away from the masses, with a view that never tires. A place to spend the day eating, drinking and lazing on their XL-sunbeds, free of charge if you spend over 30 euro (which isn't too difficult). Live music on Saturday and Sunday afternoons from 2 to 4 pm.

324 BAOBAB SUITES

C/ Roques del
Salmor 5
Costa Adeje
+34 822 070 030
baobabsuites.com

This modern vanguard hotel that has a glamorous feel to it, enjoys a top location within the de luxe five-star hotel zone. Their BB bar/restaurant has an elegant outdoor terrace, perfect for a relaxing drink whilst overlooking what has become Tenerife's largest and most popular tourist area. It's hard to believe that less than 50 years ago nothing of this infrastructure in the South even existed.

SUNSETS *at the chiringuitos*

325 CHIRINGUITO PIRATA
Paseo Sotavento - La Tejita s/n
El Médano
+34 659 557 020
chiringuito-pirata. business.site

Try the *ceviche* or other fresh seafood dishes at this popular beach shack loved by the natives. Notice their daily and wise one-liners on the blackboard: 'Breathe, it's only a bad day, not a bad life'. Weekends get busy with happy people enjoying good music, lovely food, cool beer, great vibes and magical sunsets.

326 MANA NUI CHIRINGUITO
C/ Aquiles –
Montaña Amarilla
Costa del Silencio

Facing the imposing Yellow Mountain, this tucked-in-the-rock *chiringuito* is ideal for its natural juices, refreshing mojitos and barbecue options, while you sunbathe or chill on the rocks. Frequented by locals, this area is famous for its crystal clear turquoise waters, with vertical ladder stairs helping you in and out of the sea.

327 COQUELUCHE

**Paseo de la
Pedrera – Playa la
Enramada
Costa Adeje
+34 922 71 54 83**

Join the cheerful crowd at this first-line seafront wooden *cabaña*. Sit with your toes in the sand, a cocktail in your hand and take pleasure in the colourful sunsets. If you're hungry grab a snack or a pasta and watch the occasional parasailer glide by and land in front of you. Good live-music on most afternoons.

327 COQUELUCHE

CLUBBING *with the locals*

328 ACHAMAN DISCOPUB
Av. Bruselas,
Entrada Playa
Fañabe
Fañabe
+34 922 712 159

A huge and well-designed Latino nightclub with inviting outdoor terraces, indoor dancing areas and even a few pool tables. If you love *reggaetón*, *merengue*, *salsa* and *bachata* and are keen on meeting a few good-looking locals, you'll love it here. Wednesday nights are special with live Latin-music events.

329 PAPAGAYO BEACH CLUB
Av. Rafael Puig y
Lluvina 2
Costa Adeje
+34 922 788 916
papagayobeachclub.com

Stay all day at this elegant overall-white beach club morphing from one scene into another. It's a cool place for breakfast, a fine-food restaurant for lunch or dinner, and come night time well-known DJ's will make you want to party into the wee hours. Thursday nights are reserved for black music; various live shows throughout the week.

330 TIBU NIGHTCLUB
C/ México, Americas
Shopping Centre
Playa de las
Américas
+34 616 793 277
tibutenerife.com

Tibu has a dark and fascinating Moroccan interior with several private VIP areas for group parties. The centric dance floor fills with people who love to dance to all kinds of music. Special Ladies' nights, Cuban, Disco, Salsa and Bachata nights add an interesting touch. Good atmosphere and great cocktails.

Multilingual **BOOKSTORES**

331 **LIBRERÍA BARBARA**

C/ Juan Pablo Abril 6
Los Cristianos
+34 922 792 301

Librería Barbara is situated in the heart of Los Cristianos. Their multilingual stock is carefully selected and very strong on books about the island, language courses and children's books. There's also a good secondhand section. Most reliable and excellent at laying their hands on whatever you are looking for.

332 **LIBRARY READING UP**

Av. Rafael Puig y Lluvina 13
Costa Adeje
+34 602 424 522
libraryreadingup. com

With a stock of around 5000 titles, in all mayor European languages, this is definitely one of Tenerife's best secondhand bookshops. Coloured stickers indicate prices; if you return your books in good condition, you obtain a 50% store credit. Further, special offers at two euro apiece will ensure you get some serious beach-reading done.

333 **TODO HOBBY LA CLAVE**

C/ Piedra Redonda 21
Los Olivos, Adeje
+34 922 710 986
todohobbylaclave.es

Considered a decent Spanish bookstore, with sadly only few foreign titles, the real highlight of this shop is their surprising additional section of musical instruments. All types of large and small guitars and strings, percussion, brass and keyboard, for sale or for rent. Look into their wide range of *timples* (Canarian string instruments).

SECONDHAND *goods*

334 SUPERPLANET

C/ Espigón del
Benchijigua 3
Los Cristianos
+34 922 752 418
superplanet.es

Tired of your CDs, DVDs or videogames? Feel like upgrading your video game platform, smartphone or tablet? Cash them in at Superplanet or exchange them for other semi-new articles you'd prefer to have, including a one year guarantee. Great place for browsing and finding what you've been searching for.

335 SURF SHOP UNDERGROUND

Centro Comercial,
Parque Santiago 2
Paseo Veracruz
Playa de las
Américas
+34 922 750 210
*surfshopsegunda
mano.com*

If you're on holiday and couldn't bring your surf stuff, shop at Underground and they'll buy it back from you at the end of your holiday. With many used surfboards and surf material to choose from, you can either buy/sell or rent. Also a good selection of secondhand skate gear. The most ecological way to use is to re-use.

336 BIKE POINT

Av. Quinto
Centenario,
Edificio Las
Terrazas
Playa de las
Américas
+34 922 796 710
bikepointtenerife.com

Bike Point, owned by three guys who are passionate about cycling, organise daily guided bike tours with many routes to choose from (to download routes see website). They also rent out all types of high quality bikes (including electric bikes), which then get sold as ex-rentals at strongly reduced prices. Highly professional. Second location in El Médano.

337 LIONS CHARITY SHOP

CC Apolo
Av. Pedro de
Bethencourt
Los Cristianos
tenerifesurlions.org

Tenerife Lions Club's motto is: 'The people who help people'. Through their two charity shops staffed by volunteers (second shop in Costa del Silencio), they raise funds and offer aid for the disadvantaged. Visit the store and there's every chance you'll snap up a bargain you didn't realise you needed.

336 BIKE POINT

The best places to
SHOP UNTIL YOU DROP

338 CENTRO COMERCIAL PLAZA DEL DUQUE

C/ Londres s/n,
Urbanización
Playa del Duque
Costa Adeje
plazadelduque.com

'The Essence of Luxury'. That's a very accurate description of this circular-shaped shopping mall. A place to look for the latest designer sunglasses, handmade soft-leather Italian bags and shoes, nicely-fitting designer clothes, which of course all come with the appropriate price tag. Check out Hissia Jewellery, fine gold and silver made by a Canarian artist using Henri Matisse patterns in some of her collections.

339 THE GOLDEN MILE

Av. de las
Américas
Playa de las
Américas

Nicknamed 'The Golden Mile', this famous avenue with its wide promenades, is an absolute shopaholic paradise in Tenerife South. Stylish high-end shopping areas combine with top-notch restaurants, pubs and cocktail bars. An enjoyable place for an evening stroll and a fair deal of people watching. Don't miss the 'dancing fountain' presenting a sound and light show at 8, 9 and 10 pm every evening.

340 SIAM MALL

Av. Siam 3
Costa Adeje
+34 922 750 252
ccsiammall.com

Siam Mall opened its doors in 2015 and instantly became a huge success. Over seventy premises represent most well-known fashion brands. There also is a good selection of restaurants, a top-level supermarket and a play area for children. Take advantage of their free shuttle service, offering four different routes covering most areas in the South.

340 SIAM MALL

Different types of **MARKETS**

341 **STREET MARKETS**

Various locations
mercadosdel
atlantico.com

If you love the hustle and bustle of street markets, the island is home to a wealth of them. Check the website to find one close to where you are staying. Our personal favourites are the cosy night market at Los Abrigos and the bohemian neo-hippy market at El Médano, which also sells good secondhand books.

342 **FARMERS' MARKETS**

(various locations)
SAN MIGUEL
FARMERS' MARKET
C/ de Miguel
Hernández Gómez
Las Chafiras
SAT/SUN: 8 AM – 2 PM
WED: 4 PM – 8 PM

Known as the island of 'eternal spring', Tenerife has incredible fresh produce all year long. Farmers' markets are an explosion of colours and smells and ideal places to stock up on the freshest of organic and artisanal goods. If you have kids, check out the San Miguel market as there is an adjoining play area and a coffee shop to relax at.

343 **FLEA MARKETS**

(various locations)
GUARGACHO
FLEA MARKET
Carretera General
Guargacho

Held on Sunday mornings, this open-air flea market is a true treasure grove if you like looking for the needle in the hay stack. Men will find a good choice of hardware and mechanical stuff to rummage through while ladies should visit stall number Q7 where the charming Jazmina might have a few secondhand designer labels in store for you.

Nice B E A C H & S W I M W E A R

344 PARADISE CANARIAN

AT: CC Plaza del
Duque, local 103
C/ Londres s/n
Costa Adeje

This recently opened spacious boutique keeps trend-hungry stylistas looking their very best while relaxing by the pool or strolling along the beach promenade. On offer: the latest exclusive swimming suits, bikinis, trunks, cool polos and shirts for him, for her and for the kids.

345 ANDREA BEACHWEAR

AT: CC El Mirador,
local 14
Av. Bruselas
Costa Adeje
+34 922 712 423
*andreabeachwear.
com*

At the five-star El Mirador hotel lies the small-scale and elegant El Mirador shopping centre with its independent little boutiques selling all kinds of original, creative and classy goods. Look for Andrea Beachwear, an exclusive shop for demanding customers, presenting many known and good-quality designer brands.

346 **COLIBRÍ**

C/ Pablos Abril 13
Los Cristianos
+34 922 792 869

Not many of us have the perfect beach-babe body and may find it hard to come across the right swimsuit or bikini. Rosa, the friendly owner of this small lingerie/beachwear shop, is extremely supportive at helping you choose what works best for you. With 33 years of experience she is a true expert within her branch and will make you feel completely at ease.

Colourful **CANARIAN**
FASHION _for special occasions_

347 **BOUTIQUE TINO**

C/ Dulce María
Loinaz 12
Los Cristianos
+34 922 793 303

Typical island fashion tends to be more colourful, flashy and revealing than northern tendencies. Experience the full colour blast at Tino's boutique, offering French and Spanish ladies' wear for special occasions. Flamboyant Tino has been in business for over 40 years at his showy little Aladdin's cave near the beach.

348 **LIBRA SHOES**

Pueblo Canario
101 & 103/104
Playa de las
Américas
+34 922 792 464
libra-shoes.com

The policy at Libra Shoes is that every grand-ceremony outfit requires a matching pair of handmade shoes and handbag, regardless of the colours and materials. With extra small and large shoesizes available, many a female has enjoyed the dramatic splendour of this dainty shop, owned by an English lady and her cat.

349 **LILOVE**

Av. Los Abrigos 1
Los Abrigos
+34 922 170 085
_lilove-moda-y-
complementos.
negocio.site_

It may look like just another clothes and accessories shop, but among locals this village fashion store is rather popular, selling outfits for all kinds of events. Why not step inside and let yourself be guided by the friendly shop assistants, who will advise you on what to wear for that special Canarian party you might be going to.

Interesting CONTEMPORARY ARCHITECTURE

350 PLAZA DE ADEJE

Plaza de España,
C/ Grande
Adeje
menis.es

Fernando Menis, whose innovative work has been acknowledged at the Museum of Modern Art in New York, equally redesigned the public town square of Adeje in 2010. This unique *plaza* grants an overwhelming view of the striking Barranco del Infierno ravine. Adjacent stands the Santa Úrsula Church, a cultural heritage site originating in the 16th century.

351 ECO-VILLAGE ITER

Polígono
Industrial de
Granadilla s/n
+34 922 747 758
casas.iter.es

This remarkable eco-village run by the Technological Institute of Renewable Energies (ITER) was built as a project to create bioclimatic homes, adapted to the local climate and self-sufficient in their energy needs. Architects from around the globe submitted many original ideas and 25 houses were selected from 397 entries. These very exceptional houses can be visited or even rented, as long as you don't mind the accompanying swish of the surrounding giant wind turbines.

350 **PLAZA DE ADEJE**

352 MAGMA ART & CONGRESS

Av. de los Pueblos s/n
Playa de las Américas
+34 922 752 027
tenerifemagma.com

This exciting infrastructure, inaugurated in 2005, simulates the waves of the sea and is one of architect Fernando Menis' masterpieces. Built in concrete and the local *chasnera* volcanic stone, it is a modern venue boasting fantastic acoustics, where many musical and cultural events take place. Guided tours of the building are available.

352 MAGMA ART & CONGRESS

Routes for CYCLING, MOUNTAIN BIKING and HORSE RIDING

353 BIKE EXPERIENCE TENERIFE

Av. Quinto Centenario 2, local 5
Playa de las Américas
+34 922 088 188
bikeexperience tenerife.com

Knowing the best corners of the island is a huge asset. Check out the website and, depending on the amount of effort you are prepared to put in, decide which track to follow. At Bike Experience different types of bicycles can be rented in order to train and explore either by yourself or in a guided group.

354 LAVATRAX TENERIFE

+34 646 111 223
lavatrax.com

Tenerife is a unique place for mountain biking. The North boasts world-class trails in a humid subtropical forest whereas the South will see you riding on volcanic ash in desert-like environments. Remember though: biking along Teide National Park's hiking trails is a strict no-no. Contact Darran at Lavatrax to show you where to get the best experiences.

355 HORSE TREKKING

AT: Hotel La Casona del Patio
C/ La Iglesia 68
Santiago del Teide
+34 922 839 293
ginestarhotels.com

This small-scale stable belongs to Hotel La Casona del Patio. It organises guided horse treks across the unique and strange surroundings of the Chinyero volcano and through the fragrant Canarian pine woods. Depending on age and riding experience they offer anything between 10-minute mounts on a pony to 3-hour rides down spectacular paths.

CLIMB A VOLCANO

and relish the views

---

356 YELLOW MOUNTAIN NATURAL MONUMENT (71 M)

C/ Eneas 2
Costa del Silencio

Here you will find one of the island's most unusual landscapes, highlighted by a fossil dune at the foot of the structure. A clearly-marked footpath, going up the mountain and bordering it, will show you the way. Make sure to bring your swimming gear as the crystalline waters in this area are extremely luring. After having worked up a climbers' sweat, a cool Dorada beer will go down well at the nearby Mana Nui Chiringuito.

357 RED MOUNTAIN SPECIAL NATURE RESERVE (171 M)

C/ El Cano 9
El Médano

Perfect for a family outing. Older kids will find the walk up to the summit a fairly easy challenge while smaller children will love the nearby sandy beach and the many rockpools at the base of the mountain. If you like birdwatching, take your binoculars as the surrounding Special Nature Reserve is an excellent spot for observing migratory marine and aquatic birds.

358 GUAZA MOUNTAIN NATURAL MONUMENT (429 M)

Guaza

This awesome volcanic dome is accessible from both Los Cristianos and El Palm-Mar. On your path you'll encounter abandoned stone quarries and extended plains where in the old days farmers planted their crops. One last tip: if you're a strong climber consider conquering the granddaddy of them all: Mount Roque del Conde (999 m) with its unrivalled 360-degree panoramic views of the south of the island.

356 YELLOW MOUNTAIN

WATER ACTIVITIES
for the energetic

---

359 SNORKELLING
Playa del Puertito de Adeje
38678 Costa Adeje

With the latest no-tube-in-the-mouth snorkelling masks this diversion has become exceedingly popular. Try your luck at El Puertito, a small bay north of Adeje, famous for its giant turtles and rays. The impressive turtles are known to swim right up to you and even to let you stroke them. In between exploring dips, visit the local bar for a cool drink or something nice to eat.

360 STAND-UP PADDLE, SURF AND KAYAK
Nautilos Sup
C/ Los Guíos, Playa de los Gigantes
Los Gigantes
+34 922 860 965
nautilossup.com

The steep giant cliffs of Los Gigantes provide an impressive backdrop to try out paddle surf and kayak, which are fun and low-difficulty sea activities. No need to join an excursion because here you can rent out the required material and take off on your own, in search of the many whales and dolphins that occupy these waters.

361 WIND & KITESURF
Tenerife Kitesurf
Paseo Nuestra Señora Mercedes de Rojas 58
El Médano
+34 922 179 177
tenerifekitesurf.es

For onlookers the colourful show of kites gliding through the air is captivating, but for wind and kite surfers El Médano beach is holy. With its surf-perfect air currents, it is a Mecca for those wanting to master wind and waves. Get geared up at Tenerife Kitesurf and join the lively surf scene.

360 **STAND-UP PADDLE**

362 **PLAYA DE TAJAO**

C/ Callao Hondo
San Miguel de
Tajao

Tajao is an unspoilt example of where to find the original spirit of small fishing communities on the island. Do some exploring around this fairly unexploited area and you will be rewarded with surprisingly private and hidden bathing spots. Finish off the day at one of Tajao's famous restaurants serving the best fresh fish and seafood in Tenerife.

363 **PLAYA DE LA TEJITA**

TF-643
La Tejita

If you like an all-over tan without the strap marks, a long golden beach with perfect waves, an idyllic setting against a red mountain, and tons of space to share with very few people, you should try out La Tejita. Situated on the east coast, it tends to be quite breezy, so check the forecast before heading out there for a swim.

364 PLAYA DE SAN JUAN

C/ Artes de Mar
Playa San Juan

A peaceful little coastal town that has been able to keep mass tourism at bay, Playa San Juan is the ideal spot for an afternoon swim. The black sandy beach with its clean waters and its small harbour is a cool place to relax. Enjoy a coffee or a bite to eat at the flowery seafront promenade. Sunbeds and showers are available.

364 PLAYA DE SAN JUAN

Coastal STROLLS and HIKES

---

365 EL MÉDANO PROMENADE
El Médano

This is one of our favourites. It follows a sunbleached wooden path from the main plaza towards the Red Mountain. Crafty little shops, relaxing cafes, young bohemians selling their self-made jewellery, an outdoor fitness area, a stunning beach with curious rock formations, the Red Volcano and colourful kites and sails will give you plenty to see while you walk.

366 YELLOW MOUNTAIN TO AMARILLA GOLF TRAIL
Costa del Silencio

Hiking along the rugged seashore behind the Yellow Mountain will take you away from civilization and let you have an intimate experience with volcanic nature at its best. Follow the coastal trail and observe the strange and beautiful vegetation with its typical euphorbias and cacti. This satisfying hike takes more or less one hour and ends at the charming Amarilla Golf & Marina.

367 LIGHTHOUSE TRAIL OF MALPAÍS DE LA RASCA
Reserva Natural Malpaís de la Rasca Palm-Mar

This 6-km easy trail is a fabulous walk, well-suited for beginners. It takes you through a Special Nature Reserve where children particularly enjoy the many natural pools and coves strung along the way. Begin your route at Palm-Mar and follow the shore until you reach the huge red and white Rasca lighthouse. Then turn back following the same course or any of the alternative nearby paths. For a longer walk, continue until you reach Las Galletas.

366 YELLOW MOUNTAIN TO AMARILLA GOLF TRAIL

BIKING, DIVING *and* SURFING

368 BIKE POINT

Av. Quinto
Centenario, Edf.
Las Terrazas
Playa de las
Américas
+34 922 796 710
bikepointtenerife.
com

Especially during winter season well-known professional bikers teams, preparing for European summer competitions, can be seen sweating their way up the steepest mountaintops. Why not rent one of the latest carbon fibre racing bikes or join a guided cycling tour at Bike Point, to feel what it's like conquering Mount Teide on wheels and pedals. Second location in El Médano.

369 DIVING TENERIFE SCUBA

Club Marino Hotel
C/ Minerva 2
Costa del Silencio
+34 922 785 584
divingtenerifescuba.
com

Tenerife really comes to life underwater with its spectacular volcanic scenery and its bountiful variety of friendly marine life often changing with the seasons. Tenerife Scuba, a family-run and friendly diving centre, looks after both novice and experienced divers in a club-like atmosphere. Free pick-up and drop-off service is available.

370 OCEAN LIFE TENERIFE SURF SCHOOL

AT: **CC Parque Santiago 2, local 29 Av. Rafael Puig Lluvina Playa de las Américas**

Choosing a good surf instructor from a wide range of surf centres is not an easy task, but longhaired Jaime at Ocean Life Tenerife is simply one of the best. Learn how to ride the ocean's waves in a small group or on a one-to-one basis and be taught the necessary tips by this laidback professional. Once you get the hang of it, equipment can be further rented.

Find out **WHAT LIVES IN THE OCEAN**

371 **CHARTER A YACHT**

AT: **Destio Charter Tenerife**
Puerto Colon, dock 2
Playa de las Américas
+34 633 277 441
destio.eu

If you like living in the lap of luxury, enjoy exquisite food and want to explore life in and around the ocean, chartering a yacht that provides gastronomy at sea might make your heart leap. Stefaan, your personal chef on board, prepares lobster fit for a king. Book either completely private or by seat, as part of a group of maximum eight people.

372 **HIRE A TRANSPARENT KAYAK**

START AT: **Eco-Tours Tenerife**
Av. de los Playeros, Los Cristianos Beach
Los Cristianos
+34 606 589 618
ecotourstenerife.com

This insanely cool, rather genius transparent kayak is the perfect gizmo for those who want to take a paddle and see what's beneath them. Getting any closer to the magnificent dolphins, pilot whales, turtles and fish without a full submersion is practically impossible. A low-budget, exciting and original way to soak in all the under-the-sea magic.

373 GO ON THE YELLOW SUBMARINE

**38639 Marina
San Miguel**
+34 922 736 629
*submarinesafaris.
com*

Worldwide there are only 16 submarines dedicated to tourism, of which the Sub Fun Cinco with a capacity of 44 passengers, operates in Tenerife. An interesting family outing and probably the only activity in which you can see manta rays without having to get your hair wet. For safety reasons children under two are not allowed on board.

MODERN ART *in the South*

374 MARIPOSA

C/ Túnez 63-A
Arona
+34 922 726 232
*kulturpark-
mariposa.de*

This singular art project came to life in 1993 by German gallery owners Hans-Jürgen and Helga Müller. Over the next 20 years, together with 80 artists from all over the world, they created a unique and captivating domain strewn with modern works of arts, a dazzling golden stairway, little plazas, viewpoints, exhibit rooms and original accommodation options. Visits upon request only.

375 LA MUSA

C/ Grande 22
Adeje
+34 618 888 897
lamusadeadeje.com

La Musa is a creative exhibition gallery as well as a painter's atelier and a place to buy contemporary arts and crafts. The showroom collaborates with different local artists enabling them to renew their collections quite often. On display are also original handmade ceramics and jewellery made of silver, natural stones and recycled materials.

376 FRANCISCO ANDRADE FUMERO PROMENADE

C/ Luis Díaz
de Losada
Playa de las
Américas

Part of what the British tend to call the 'Geranium Walk', this particular stretch of promenade accommodates a few huge monumental iron sculptures made by artists Juan López Salvador and Drago Díaz. They provide an original décor for a holiday snapshot, but also enhance the beauty of the panoramic views and the horizon line.

Famous **MUSIC FESTIVALS**

377 **FARRA WORLD MUSIC FESTIVAL**
farraworld.com

Not only Ibiza or Tomorrowland play the best electronic sounds. Large numbers of 'party people' have started to flock to the sunny island to witness the world's best DJs at work. The increasingly popular Farra World Music Festival is spread out over various happenings. Beware: tickets sell out in two shakes of a lamb's tail.

377 **FARRA WORLD MUSIC FESTIVAL**

C

378 ARONA SUMMER FESTIVAL

**Amarilla Golf &
38639 Marina
San Miguel**
*aronasummer
festival.com*

Since 2011, this is Tenerife's highlight of the electronic festival scene. Internationally renowned artists such as David Guetta, deadmau5 and Steve Aoki have been welcomed here. This two-day event takes place on the grounds of the Amarilla Golf & Marina, where partygoers can put up their tents and enjoy the sun, the sea, the music and the good vibes.

379 CANARIAS JAZZ & MÁS HEINEKEN

canariasjazz.com

The Canary Islands' International Jazz Festival, which had its first edition in 1994, is held in a series of venues throughout the islands. The programme includes performances by musicians ranging from promising newcomers to leading national and international musicians. Jazz lovers should also check out Red Mountain Jazz Festival (jazzroja.com) operating on a much smaller scale but offering high-quality music.

RURAL and **COSY** hideaways

380 **LA CASONA DEL PATIO**

C/ de la Iglesia 68
Santiago del Teide
+34 922 839 293
ginestarhotels.com

If you enjoy the great outdoors, are into walking and horse riding, then this is definitely the place for you. Part of the hotel dates back to the 17th century presenting some interesting displays of days gone by. Plan your visit in January/February as you will then witness this valley becoming fairy-like with its sea of delicately blooming almond trees.

381 **LA CASONA SANTO DOMINGO**

C/ Santo Domingo 32
Güímar
+34 922 510 229
casonasanto domingo.com

This traditional 17th-century manor house, preserving its wooden beams and original flooring, is owned by the French Nathalie, who has blessed it with her fine touch. They serve Canarian cuisine with a twist while their pleasant flower-filled inner patio, is a relaxing spot to indulge in a good book and a cool drink.

382 **FINCA SALAMANCA**

Ctra. Güímar,
El Puertito 2
Güímar
+34 922 514 530
hotel-finca salamanca.com

Rural hotel Salamanca is the perfect tranquil hidey-hole. Far away from the commotion and surrounded by well-kept and outstanding gardens, this is a great venue to switch off. Other bonusses are their little heated pool and their famous restaurant situated in an old tobacco barn, where high-standard Canarian food and wines are served.

PURE LUXURY

away from the crowds

383 HOTEL SPA VILLALBA

Camino San Roque
s/n
Vilaflor
+34 922 709 930
hotelvillalba.com

At 1600-metre altitude and completely surrounded by the fragrant pine forest, we are looking at a romantic mountain getaway. This relaxing adults-only Spa Hotel with its big windows and huge no-clutter rooms is the perfect setting to listen to birdsong, to gaze at the clearest starry skies and to inhale the purest of unpolluted air.

384 ABAMA RESORT

Ctra. General del
Sur, TF-47, km 9
Guía de Isora
+34 922 126 011
abamahotelresort.
com

By no means a cheap place to stay, but worth every penny to be able to enjoy what is considered the best hotel on the island. Expect peace and privacy, unusual architecture, Michelin-starred food, a good game of golf, a secluded beach and breathtaking views. This is Tenerife's Ritz Carlton, a place where famous actors, sports people and politicians can be spotted.

385 ROYAL GARDEN VILLAS & SPA

C/ Alcojora s/n
Costa Adeje
+34 922 711 294
royalgardenvillas.
com

Set in exotic flower-scented gardens and decorated in a rich Asian style, this luxurious boutique hotel comprises 28 de luxe villas. Every villa has its own private pool and their in-house Spa service is very highly rated. Should you care for a break from the exquisite indulgence, this chic retreat is relatively close to the livelier areas of Costa Adeje.

OUT-OF-THE-BOX

places to stay

386 LOS AMIGOS HOSTEL

C/ Giralda 9
La Mareta (Los Abrigos)
El Médano
+34 922 749 320
losamigoshostels.com

This walled villa with its outdoor pool and comfy relax area is the perfect hostel for young backpackers (and the young at heart!) who enjoy a friendly laidback atmosphere far away from mass tourism. Choose either a shared room, a private room or a tent in the garden. Breakfast and lockers are included; evening meals are vegetarian.

387 ECO-VILLAGE ITER

Polígono Industrial de Granadilla s/n
+34 922 747 758
casas.iter.es

These bioclimatic, futuristic and experimental houses, also mentioned under 'Interesting Contemporary Architecture', are priceless eye-openers for those who respect the environment and are curious about renewable energy. Every house, fitted with stunning designer interiors, is totally exclusive. The project is situated next to the sea, within a technology park adjoining the Natural Monument Montaña Pelada.

388 HACIENDA CRISTÓFORO

C/ El Horno 10
Playa Paraiso
+34 922 741 967
haciendacristoforo.
com

There is nothing to compare the Hacienda with, because of its extreme uniqueness. The complex was conceived and gradually built over the years by Denis, an old and wise Greek spiritual architect, still living on the premises. This heavenly peaceful paradise is often used as a yoga and meditation retreat centre.

388 HACIENDA CRISTÓFORO

VISIT A SPA

and relax with a massage

389 AQUA CLUB TERMAL

C/ Galicia 6
Torvisca Alto,
Costa Adeje
+34 922 979 287
aquaclubtermal.com

Loosen up every muscle in your body at the biggest spa in Tenerife. Relish different types of massages, pools, showers, steam baths and a sauna, with normal thermal circuits lasting 2,5 hours. Also check out their VIP circuits, Night Spa breaks and Nudist Nights, allowing complete relaxation without the nuisance of a swimsuit.

390 HOTEL SENSIMAR LOS GIGANTES SPA

C/ Flor de Pascua 8
Los Gigantes
+34 922 861 020
stilhotels.com
>sensimar los gigantes

This small and scented spa centre offers a good one-hour water circuit deal at only 10 euro per person. The main focus though is on their expert team of manicurists, beauticians and masseurs. Ask for the 'couples massage' deal including a bottle of cava, chocolate truffles, a 50-minute massage and unlimited use of the thermal circuit.

391 MARYLANZA SUITES & SPA

C/ Los Arenales 20
Los Cristianos
+34 922 787 816
marylanza.com
spacio10.es

Wallowing in this exceptionally romantic spa will de-stress your mind and body in a tranquil way. Afterwards you can combine the benefits of the water with some extra soothing wellness, or with an invigorating fitness workout at their Spacio 10 gym, which is one of the most modern and fully equipped gyms in the South.

FUN PARKS *for the whole family*

392 MONKEY PARK

Camino Moreque-
Llano Azul 17
Los Cristianos
+34 922 790 720
monkeypark.com

A reproduction centre for endangered species, this small zoo is many children's favourite. Buy a little bag of animal food at the entrance so you can feed the monkeys, tortoises, iguanas, guinea pigs, etc. Best of all are the walk-in cages where playful titi monkeys or curious lemurs come and sit on your head.

393 CAMEL PARK

Ctra. General
Los Cristianos –
La Camella s/n
La Camella
+34 922 721 121
camelpark.es

The single humped dromedaries, brought to the Canary Islands in the 16th century, were very important domestic animals for agriculture and transport. With the arrival of tourism in the sixties, they became less relevant and started being used for tourist purposes. Various camel farms dotted around the island will let you experience a ride on them.

394 ECOLOGICAL FARM EL CARRETÓN

Camino del
Carretón s/n
Arafo, Güímar
+34 922 513 979
fincaelcarreton.com

Unknown to many, this authentic ecological farm organises fun guided visits. Kids are free to feed and to interact with the domestic farm animals. They can watch the goats being milked and even enjoy a ride on the mini ponies. Stay for lunch and try their Cuban inspired cuisine or their original tapas. Arrange your visit by phone beforehand.

ANAGA MOUNTAINS

INDEX

COLOPHON

EDITING *and* COMPOSING – Conny Melkebeek —
connychristine@gmail.com

GRAPHIC DESIGN – Joke Gossé

PHOTOGRAPHY – Sergio Villalba — www.sergiovillalba.com

COVER IMAGE – Tensei Tenmoku (secret 238)

The addresses in this book have been selected after thorough independent research by the author, in collaboration with Luster Publishers. The selection is solely based on personal evaluation of the business by the author. Nothing in this book was published in exchange for payment or benefits of any kind.

D/2018/12.005/8
ISBN 978 94 6058 2219
NUR 512, 510

© 2018, Luster, Antwerp
www.lusterweb.com
info@lusterweb.com

Printed in Italy by Printer Trento.

MIX
Paper from responsible sources
FSC® C015829

All rights reserved.
No part of this publication may be reproduced, stored in a retrieval system, or transmitted, in any form or by any means, without the prior written consent of the publisher. An exception is made for short excerpts, which may be cited for the sole purpose of reviews.